Thucydides

ANCIENTS IN ACTION

Boudicca
Marguerite Johnson

Catiline
Barbara Levick

Catullus
Amanda Hurley

Cleopatra
Susan Walker and Sally-Ann Ashton

Hadrian
James Morwood

Hannibal
Robert Garland

Horace
Philip D. Hills

Lucretius
John Godwin

Martial
Peter Howell

Ovid: Love Songs
Genevieve Lively

Ovid: Myth and Metamorphosis
Sarah Annes Brown

Pindar
Anne Pippin Burnett

Sappho
Marguerite Johnson

Spartacus
Theresa Urbainczyk

Tacitus
Rhiannon Ash

Thucydides

P. J. Rhodes

Bloomsbury Academic
An imprint of Bloomsbury Publishing Plc

BLOOMSBURY
LONDON • NEW DELHI • NEW YORK • SYDNEY

Bloomsbury Academic
An imprint of Bloomsbury Publishing Plc

50 Bedford Square 1385 Broadway
London New York
WC1B 3DP NY 10018
UK USA

www.bloomsbury.com

BLOOMSBURY and the Diana logo are trademarks of Bloomsbury Publishing Plc

First published 2015

© P. J. Rhodes, 2015

P. J. Rhodes has asserted his right under the Copyright, Designs and Patents Act, 1988, to be identified as Author of this work.

All rights reserved. No part of this publication may be reproduced or transmitted in any form or by any means, electronic or mechanical, including photocopying, recording, or any information storage or retrieval system, without prior permission in writing from the publishers.

No responsibility for loss caused to any individual or organization acting on or refraining from action as a result of the material in this publication can be accepted by Bloomsbury or the author.

British Library Cataloguing-in-Publication Data
A catalogue record for this book is available from the British Library.

ISBN: PB: 978-1-47252-399-0
ePDF: 978-1-47252-658-8
ePub: 978-1-47252-207-8

Library of Congress Cataloging-in-Publication Data
A catalog record for this book is available from the Library of Congress.

Series: Ancients in Action

Typeset by Fakenham Prepress Solutions, Fakenham, Norfolk NR21 8NN
Printed and bound in India

Contents

Preface..vi
References to Ancient Texts...............vii
Principal Dates...ix
Map: The World of Thucydides...............xi

1 The World of Thucydides.....................1
2 Thucydides the Historian...................11
3 Thucydides the Thinker.......................51
4 After Thucydides.....................................71

Further Reading...87
Index..91

Preface

My thanks to Dr R. D. Rees and to the staff of Bloomsbury for inviting me to write this book and encouraging me as I worked on it. This series of books, Ancients in Action, 'introduces major figures of the ancient world to the modern general reader, including the essentials of each subject's life, works and significance for later western civilisation'. I hope that my book will be found interesting and worthwhile by students as well as by 'the modern general reader', and will encourage readers of both kinds to read and enjoy Thucydides, and I end the book with a guide to further reading, but the publishers did not want and I have not set out to provide a textbook.

I have been involved with Thucydides for many years, and inevitably I say some things in this book which I have said previously elsewhere, in different ways and on different levels for different audiences. In particular I thank Oxbow Books (successors to Aris and Phillips) for permission to adapt material from my editions of books I, II, III and IV. 1–V. 24, and Oxford University Press for permission to adapt material from my Introduction to and Notes on the Oxford World's Classics translation of Thucydides by M. Hammond. All translations are my own, apart from the quotations on p. 84.

References to Ancient Texts

References by numbers alone (e.g. I. 2. iii–iv) are to Thucydides. For other texts I use the following abbreviations:

Arist. *Pol.*	Aristotle, *Politics*
Ath. *Pol.*	*Athenaion Politeia* (the *Athenian Constitution* written in Aristotle's school)
CIL	*Corpus Inscriptionum Latinarum*
Diod. Sic.	Diodorus Siculus
FGrH	F. Jacoby et al. (eds), *Die Fragmente der griechischen Historiker*
Fornara	C. W. Fornara (ed.), *Translated Documents of Greece and Rome*, i. *Archaic Times to the Peloponnesian War* (Cambridge University Press, ²1983)
Hdt.	Herodotus
ILS	*Inscriptiones Latinae Selectae*
Lewis and Reinhold³	N. Lewis and M. Reinhold, *Roman Civilization* (Columbia University Press, ³1990).
Lucian, *Hist. Conscr.*	Lucian, *Quomodo Historia Conscribenda sit* (*How History should be Written*)
M&L	R. Meiggs and D. M. Lewis (eds), *A Selection of Greek Historical Inscriptions to the End of the Fifth Century* B.C. (Oxford University Press, 1968)

Pl. *Resp.*	Plato, *Respublica* (*Republic*)
Plin. *H.N.*	Pliny, *Historia Naturalis*
Plut. *Per.*	Plutarch, *Pericles*
PSI	*Pubblicazioni della Società Italiana per la Ricerca dei Papiri Greci e Latini in Egitto*
Sen. *Controvers.*	Seneca, *Controversiae*
Smallwood, *Docs. ... Gaius*	E. M. Smallwood (ed.), *Documents Illustrating the Principates of Gaius, Claudius and Nero* (Cambridge University Press, 1967)
Tac. *Ann.*	Tacitus, *Annals*
Vell. Pat.	Velleius Paterculus
[Xen.]	Xenophon [attributed to]

Principal Dates

(*Dates in the form 478/7 are either Athenian official years, beginning in midsummer, or from 431 onwards Thucydidean years, beginning in spring*)

499–493	Ionian Revolt against Persia
490	Persian invasion of Greece (battle of Marathon)
480–479	Persian invasion of Greece (battles of Thermopylae, Artemisium, Salamis, Plataea)
478/7	foundation of Delian League
c. 460	**birth of Thucydides**
c. 460–446	First Peloponnesian War
440–439	Athens' war against Samos
435–433	war between Corinth and Corcyra
432	Athens' attack on Potidaea
431	Thebes' attack on Plataea
431	**beginning of Peloponnesian War**
430–427/6	plague in Athens
429	battles in Gulf of Corinth, aborted Spartan attack on Piraeus
428–427	revolt of Mytilene against Athens
427	capitulation of Plataea to Sparta
427–425	civil war in Corcyra
427–424	Athens' campaign in Sicily
426	Athens' defeat in Aetolia
426/5	campaign in north-western Greece
425	Athens' success at Pylos
424	Athens' capture of Cythera
424	Athens' unsuccessful attack on Megara

424/3	Athens' defeat by Boeotians at Delium
424–422	campaign to north-west of Aegean
423	one-year truce between Athens and Sparta
421	**Peace of Nicias**
420	Athens' alliance with Argos and other Peloponnesians
418	Sparta's victory over Athens and allies at Mantinea
416	Athens' capture of Melos
415	religious scandals at Athens
415–413	Athens' major campaign in Sicily
413	Sparta's occupation of Decelea
412	Sparta's first alliance with Persia
411	oligarchic revolutions in Athens
411 autumn	**end of Thucydides' narrative**
410	Athens' victory over Sparta at Cyzicus
406	Sparta's victory over Athens at Notium
406	Athens' victory over Sparta at Arginusae
405	Sparta's victory over Athens at Aegospotami
404	**Athens' capitulation, end of Peloponnesian War**
c. 400	death of Thucydides

The World of Thucydides

1

The World of Thucydides

Thucydides, the Athenian historian, lived from about 460 B.C. to a little after 404, and wrote a history of the Peloponnesian War, the war between Athens and Sparta, at the time the two most powerful states in Greece, which began in 431 and ended with Spartan victory in 404. Although there are a few allusions to the end of the war, he did not live to finish his history, but the narrative breaks off in the autumn of 411. The war was important, because, as Thucydides says, it was long drawn out (I. 23. i), and most of the Greek world, together with some non-Greek peoples, were caught up in it (I. 1. i–ii), though it did not finally settle the rivalry between Athens and Sparta, which continued into the fourth century. Thucydides' history of the war is important, because he lived through it and was involved in it, and because his history has impressed readers as a work of exceptional thoroughness and intellectual calibre, and it has been admired ever since, both in antiquity and in more recent times.

In it he sought not only to establish what happened but also to explain how and why it happened, writing:

> To the listener its lack of a fabulous element will perhaps make it less attractive; but if it is judged useful by those who want to examine a clear account of what happened, the like of which or similar things will in the course of human nature some time happen again, that will suffice.

Not lacking in confidence, he continued:

> What I have written is a possession for all time rather than a competition piece for immediate hearing (I. 22. iv)

– and reactions to his work have shown that his confidence was justified. However, we shall see that, as fashions in scholarship have changed, the ways in which Thucydides is appreciated have changed with them, and in readers' perception he has changed from being a totally dispassionate seeker after truth to being an engaged writer who used his considerable skill to lead readers to see what had happened as he wanted.

The Greek World

The first great civilisations of the Greek world flourished in the bronze age of the second millennium B.C.: the Minoan, based on the island of Crete, the Cycladic, based on the islands of the southern Aegean, and the Mycenaean, based on the southern part of the Greek mainland. The Mycenaeans were Greeks linguistically: that is, their written texts (clay tablets used for administrative record-keeping, in the script known as Linear B) show that their language was a version of the language used by the Greeks in the first millennium. By the beginning of the first millennium those civilisations had broken down, and the Greek world was comparatively thinly populated, isolated and primitive. By the end of the first millennium the Greek world had been absorbed into the empire of Rome.

Between c. 800 and c. 500 there developed a new Greek civilisation, intellectually and artistically lively and politically innovative, and renewing the Greeks' contacts with and indeed expanding into the wider Mediterranean world, until there were settlements of Greeks established from the western Mediterranean to the Black Sea and Egypt. The bronze-age civilisations seem to have been organised in large kingdoms, but after their collapse life was based on separate, small communities, and such communities remained the norm in the first millennium, both in the Greeks' heartland

and in their settlements overseas. In some areas local communities with less independence were grouped in a regional entity, but most of the local communities became *poleis* (commonly translated as 'city states': most were so small that the word 'city' may give a false impression, but for convenience I shall refer to them as cities here), communities which aspired to a high degree of independence and to self-government through their body of (adult male native-born) citizens. By c. 500 there were about 1,000 of these altogether, about 700 of them in mainland Greece, the Aegean and its northern and eastern coasts.

Thucydides himself provides a short account of this development, in an introduction designed to show that the Greeks of his time were more powerful and the Peloponnesian War was a greater war than in the past (I. 1–23. iii). Legends about the Greeks' past were located in the world of the bronze-age civilisations, and there was no awareness of the collapse of those civilisations and the new beginning which followed, so that he argues for a simple progression from primitive beginnings via the bronze age to the heights reached in his own time.

Athens and Sparta were both unusual in that each came to control directly a much larger territory than was controlled by most Greek cities. Sparta was supreme in its own area of Laconia (in the south of the Peloponnese, the southern part of the Greek mainland) and in Messenia, to the west of that, a total area of about 2,400 sq. miles = 6,200 km². Within that area the Spartans proper were a privileged minority (about 8,000 adult males at the beginning of the fifth century, declining to 1,000 or fewer by the middle of the fourth); of the other inhabitants some were *perioikoi* ('those living around'), free members of their own communities but subordinate to Sparta, others were 'helots', (a word which perhaps means 'captives' or 'slaves'), in a state of serfdom. The large subject population made it both possible and necessary for the Spartans to adopt a full-time military life. Athens was the one city in the whole of Attica, about 1,000 sq. miles

= 2,600 km^2, but Athenian citizens lived throughout Attica in more than 100 separate communities, which became 'demes' (local units) of the city of Athens rather than separate cities in their own right. There were perhaps 60,000 adult male citizens at the beginning of the Peloponnesian War and 30,000 at the end; and also, in addition to the citizens' families, significant numbers of 'metics' (migrants who lived in Attica, for a time or permanently, but had not been made citizens) and chattel slaves, who were the property of the citizens and metics who owned them.

Sparta, after conquering Messenia in the eighth and seventh centuries, did not in the sixth century manage to make further conquests, but managed to build up a network of alliances – which we refer to as the Peloponnesian League – by which most other Peloponnesian cities accepted Sparta's leadership. The most important exception was Argos, in the north-east of the Peloponnese, which was never willing to acknowledge Sparta's superiority. Athens, which considered itself to be the mother city of the Ionian Greeks, who had settled in many of the Aegean islands and part of coastal Asia Minor, enjoyed a new burst of energy and confidence after the overthrow (with Spartan help) in 510 of a family of 'tyrants' (men who usurped power) which had ruled the city for some decades.

The leading power in the near east was Persia, which in the second half of the sixth century had extended its control to the Aegean coast of Asia Minor and had made the Greek cities there and on the islands near the coast subject to it. In the 490s those cities rose against Persia in the Ionian Revolt, with some help from Athens and from Eretria, on the island of Euboea. The revolt was suppressed, and the involvement of Athens and Eretria gave the Persians the stimulus and the excuse to cross the Aegean and attack Greece. In 490 they captured Eretria and deported much of the population, but the Athenians defeated them at Marathon. In 480–479 they returned with larger forces. Sparta was accepted as the leader of the Greeks who joined in opposing them (not all did); Athens, which had spent the profits from its silver mines on enlarging its navy, provided more than half of the ships; and after beginning successfully the Persians were again defeated. For a year the Spartans remained in command as the Greeks began to fight back against the Persians, but after that the fighting was continued by Athens at the head of an alliance of Aegean and Asiatic Greeks, referred to as the Delian League because its headquarters was the sacred island of Delos. Athens became increasingly domineering, coercing allies who were reluctant to contribute year after year, and after a time nearly all the allies were making cash payments ('tribute', recalling the tribute collected by the Persians from their subjects) rather than contributing their own forces to joint campaigns. About the middle of the century regular campaigning against Persia ended, but the League, looking more and more like an empire, was kept in existence.

Increasingly the Greek world came to be polarised between Sparta with its mainland Peloponnesian League and Athens with its maritime Delian League. Athens, whose naval power meant that the poorer citizens, who rowed the ships, mattered more for their city's success than in other cities, had taken the final steps to a democracy (the word was probably coined in the first half of the fifth century with reference to Athens) in which even the poorer citizens had significant political power, while Sparta's citizens were a small minority among their region's population, and so Athens came to be seen as a champion of democracy and Sparta of oligarchy. In Athens in the fifth century, literature (particularly drama) and various arts flourished, while Sparta came to pride itself on an old-fashioned simplicity. Athens was expansive, while Sparta was more concerned to keep what it already had. There was fighting between the two leagues in the 450s and early 440s (in the so-called First Peloponnesian War), which ended with a treaty by which Athens gave up what it had gained on the mainland; but Athens' appetite for expansion was unchecked. There was not room in the Greek world for both an expanding Athens and an undiminished Sparta, and episodes in which Athens, if not formally in breach of the treaty, was at any rate not anxious to avoid provocation, led Sparta and the Peloponnesian League to declare war on Athens in 431, with the stated object of freeing the Greeks from Athenian domination. That is the war – the Peloponnesian War as we call it, the war between the Athenians and the Peloponnesians as Thucydides called it (I. 1. i) – of which Thucydides set out from its beginning to write the history.

Literature and Philosophy

The writing of history was not yet long established when Thucydides wrote. Epic poems, of which the *Iliad* and *Odyssey* attributed to Homer survive, told stories about what the Greeks believed to be their distant past. There was a body of such stories, which poets of various kinds could draw on and adapt: among them, early in the fifth century, Pindar, a lyric poet from Boeotia (north of Attica), who wrote for patrons in various places; and for much of the fifth century the Athenian writers of tragedy, represented for us by Aeschylus, Sophocles and Euripides. These were stories in which the leading families were descended from gods, and gods were imagined in the likeness of human beings, behaved and misbehaved like human beings and sometimes intervened in the affairs of human beings. Soon after the Persian Wars Simonides, active at the beginning of the fifth century, wrote a poem in which those wars were compared with the legendary Greek war against Troy.

In the sixth century, particularly in the cities of coastal Asia Minor, philosophers had emerged who took a very different kind of interest in the world, rejecting the anthropomorphic gods of the poets, if not gods of any kind, and trying to explain in other ways how the cosmos began and how it worked, and what principles should underlie human behaviour in the cosmos and in cities and other human communities. That paved the way for accounts of human activities written in human terms rather than divine terms, and in prose rather than verse. Hecataeus, of Miletus (in Asia Minor), active c. 500, wrote an account of the places and peoples one would find on a journey round the Mediterranean and the Black Sea, and the *Genealogies*, trying to elicit the truth behind the legends of various families. His work is known only from quotations and allusions.

We do, however, have the history of Herodotus, of Halicarnassus (again in Asia Minor), written between the 440s and the 420s. He seems to represent a significant advance on Hecataeus. He wrote 'so that the deeds of men should not be lost in time and that great and wonderful achievements of Greeks and barbarians should not become unknown' (Hdt. I. preface), with particular reference to the wars between the Greeks and Persians at the beginning of the fifth century. Before he reaches those wars (which occupy the second half of his work) he manages to include information on various Greek and non-Greek communities and their history, in the previous two or three centuries; divine plans are present, but only to add a further dimension to human explanations of human events; the legendary past is quickly dismissed (Hdt. I. 1–5), and within more recent history he draws some kind of line about the middle of the sixth century, which was as far back as the oldest people he spoke to will themselves have remembered. The result is not, of course, the kind of book which a modern writer would have produced; but it is attractive to read, and is mature, intelligent and founded on a wide-ranging curiosity and an energetic search for material. Thucydides never refers to Herodotus by name, but he clearly knew Herodotus' work and frequently engaged with it.

In the fifth century Athens became the cultural centre of the Greek world, and it attracted men from many other cities, among them Herodotus. It also attracted men known as sophists ('wise men'), who continued the work of the sixth-century philosophers. They were willing to challenge accepted beliefs, on religion, human behaviour and much else; they were fond of contrasts such as that between nature, which is as it is and could not be otherwise, and human convention, matters which have been decided one way by human beings in one context but could be decided otherwise by others in another context, and this pointed them to relativism rather than certainty on various subjects. Many of them claimed to teach skills necessary for success in public life, such as public speaking and argument. This helped to shape the world in which Thucydides lived.

Thucydides

Thucydides himself, born c. 460, belonged to a rich, prominent and politically active family. On both his father's side and his mother's he was descended from Miltiades, who had commanded the Athenians in their defeat of the Persians at Marathon in 490. First a son of Miltiades, Cimon, and then Thucydides' maternal grandfather, another Thucydides, in the middle of the century led the opposition to the democrats and their leader Pericles. Miltiades had spent part of his life in Thrace, to the north of the Aegean, and his wife was from there; among the few things which Thucydides tells us about himself is that he owned mining rights in Thrace and had influence with the leading men there, and (although he does not say so) it was probably on account of this that he was sent to that region when he held office as general in 424/3 (IV. 104. iv–105. i).

Athens and Sparta

A little should be said about the nature of the Athenian democracy. In Athens, as in Greek cities generally, the final decision-making body was the assembly, a mass meeting open to all adult male citizens; its business was prepared by a representative council of 500 whose membership changed each year, but it was not just a rubber stamp for the council. Administration was done not by full-time professionals but by ordinary citizens appointed to particular positions (commonly as members of a board of ten) for a year. Justice was similarly amateur and designed to involve the citizens: juries of some hundreds sat with officials who presided but did not direct; prosecution even on public matters was normally left to citizen volunteers, and prosecutors and defendants conducted their own cases. Civilian appointments, considered to require loyalty more than skill, were normally made by lot, with a ban on reappointment to the same positions; but military officers were elected and could be re-elected, and those elected to the highest position, the generalship (ten each year) often included men such as Pericles, who were politically prominent. Other cities had similar structures: what varied with the complexion of the regime were the inclusion in or exclusion from the body of citizens with some political rights of the poorest men, and the balance of power betwen the ordinary citizens in the assembly and the council and officials. Athens was democratic by both of those criteria: there was no property qualification for membership of the assembly or for service on juries (but in the fifth century there still was for holding offices), and the assembly was a powerful body, not much restricted by the council, and one in which any citizens could make speeches and propose motions.

Sparta, by contrast, had two hereditary kings (allegedly descended from twins; probably in fact the result of the amalgamation of two smaller entities as the city coalesced), who commanded armies and had power inside the city as *ex officio* members of the council. There were also five ephors ('overseers'), elected annually from all full citizens with no possibility of re-election, who had probably been instituted to limit the power of the kings: they had considerable executive power, and presided in the council and assembly. The council, the *gerousia* (council of elders), comprised the two kings and 28 men aged over 60, elected for what remained of their lives from the leading families: like the Athenian council it prepared business for the assembly, but in Sparta less business reached the assembly than in Athens, and in the assembly only the kings, ephors and other members of the *gerousia* could speak and make proposals.

With helots to work their land for them, the Spartan citizens were free to cultivate a military life style; and, because they were afraid of a helot revolt, they needed to cultivate that military life style: there was an elaborate training programme for the young; adults ate in messes with their comrades, and until they reached the age of 30 slept in barracks. Economically they were not all equal, but all full citizens had land from whose produce they made contributions to their messes, and those who were unable to make their contributions were downgraded from full citizenship. The *perioikoi* were free men living in and administering their own townships, but they had to fight in the army with the Spartan citizens while having no say in the policy decisions made by the citizens. The helots were slaves, but from a subjugated element in the native population rather than chattel slaves bought individually, and their primary duty was to support the citizens by farming their land and by attending them in war. With a degree of political equality among the citizens but a much larger non-citizen population, Sparta was exceptional among the Greek cities.

2

Thucydides the Historian

The Peloponnesian War

Thucydides' text has been divided into eight books (not by himself, but this division was known to Dionysius of Halicarnassus at the end of the first century B.C.), with the books more recently subdivided into chapters and sections. Book I contains introductory material: the 'archaeology' (I. 1–23. iii), designed to show that his Greece was more powerful and his war was a greater war than in the past, and including chapters (I. 20, 22, cf. VI. 54. i) on how he set about writing his history and taking the trouble to get the details right as others do not; and an account of how the war came about (I. 23. iv–146), with a narrative of the late 430s and a digression (I. 89–118) on the growth of Athens' power during the *pentekontaetia*, the (not quite) 50 years between the Persian Wars and the Peloponnesian War, inserted to justify his belief that Athens' power and Sparta's fear of it provided the 'truest reason' for the war (I. 23. vi, 88, 118. ii). Books II–VIII provide a narrative of the years 431–411, arranged in summers of about eight months and winters of about four, and mostly keeping to chronological order (but allowing occasional departures from it for narrative convenience). The different cities had their different calendars, beginning their years at different points, and he decided that this scheme was better than any official calendar for putting events in the right contexts (II. 1–2. i, V. 20).

The war formally began in 431 with an invasion of Attica by Sparta and its Peloponnesian allies, expecting that the Athenians would face them in battle and be defeated. The Spartan king Archidamus is represented as saying to the force which invaded Attica in 431:

> We are going against a city which is in no way unable to defend itself, but is best prepared in all respects, so that we should have a strong expectation that they will come out for battle, even if they are not on the move now while we are not yet present, but when they see us in their land ravaging and destroying their property. (II. 11. vi)

But Athens was linked to its harbour at the Piraeus by 'long walls' which combined the two in a single fortified area, and Pericles' policy was not to give the invaders the battle which they wanted but to evacuate the countryside and rely on Athens' power at sea to import all that was needed:

> Pericles gave the same advice for the circumstances as before, that they should prepare for the war and bring in their things from the fields; and should not go out for battle but go into the city and guard that; and fit out their fleet, where they were strong, and keep their allies under their control. He said that their strength depended on the money received as income from their allies, and that success in most aspects of war came from good judgment and monetary superiority. (II. 13. ii)

Neither side was led to the conclusion that it could not win; in the mid 420s more adventurous policies brought some successes to Athens, but in the late 420s Sparta did better, and in 421 the war seemed to be ended by the Peace of Nicias, an attempt to return to the position of 431. Technically that was a success for Athens – Sparta's attempt to break Athens' power had failed – but a return to the position of 431 was inevitably unstable; there were problems in the implementation of the treaty, and before long war resumed. Sparta's hold on the Peloponnese was weakened, with some of its allies refusing to accept the Peace, until in 418 Athens with Argos and some other Peloponnesians brought the Spartans to a battle at Mantinea in which the Spartans were caught unprepared but were still victorious. Athens had already tried in the 420s to extend its power by intervening in a conflict in Sicily; a further ambitious attempt in 415–413 ended in disastrous failure, with the loss of many men and ships. By 413 any pretence that the Peace of Nicias was still in force had been abandoned. Sparta established a permanent fort at Decelea in the countryside of Attica, which did the Athenians more harm than the invasions at the beginning of the war had done, and it gained the support of Persia, whose resources would enable it to confront the Athenians at sea and to persevere until the Athenians were exhausted. Both sides had problems – political division in Athens when the democracy was no longer delivering success, and in Sparta between those who were willing to abandon the Greeks of Asia Minor to gain Persia's support and those who were not – but in the end in 405 Persian backing did enable Sparta to defeat Athens in a battle at Aegospotami in the Hellespont, beyond which it could not continue, and in 404 Athens capitulated.

The Composition of the History

While Herodotus was writing the history of the past – he was born a few years before the war of 480–479 with which his history culminated – Thucydides was writing of events through which he lived as an adult, and he says that he started work at the beginning of the war, expecting it to be great and particularly noteworthy (I. 1. i). He lived beyond the end of the war (II. 65. xii, V. 26. i, VI. 16. iii), though he did not manage to take his narrative beyond 411 (there is no sign that any further material was made public which has not survived for us to read, and some fourth-century historians, including Xenophon in his *Hellenica*, started their accounts where Thucydides' account ends).

How much of his history was written when used to be a problem which consumed a great deal of scholarly energy. We can be certain only that there are a few remarks which ceased to be true before the end of the war and a few allusions to later events inserted in the narrative of what happened earlier; and there are discrepancies such as that between II. 65. xi, which blames Athens' failure in Sicily in 415–413 on political weakness at home, and the impression given by the narrative in VI–VII, that the campaign could not have brought long-term success and failed in the short term because of misjudgments in Sicily. What we have is certainly not the polished and unified product of a single spell of thinking and writing. The matter is complicated by the fact that the war seemed to be ended by the Peace of Nicias in 421; but, after a period of shifting alignments and episodes which it suited the two sides not to see as putting an end to the Peace, an Athenian incursion into Laconia in 414 (VI. 105) made further pretence impossible (cf. VII. 18. ii). Thucydides marks the end of what his text as transmitted to us calls 'the first war' but may originally have called simply 'the war' in V. 24, and after mentioning the immediate sequel he has a 'second preface' in V. 25-6 to introduce the remainder of the war. This suggests that there was a time when he thought that the war had ended in 421, but later developments made him change his mind; and it is possible that during the course of his work he changed his mind on other matters, about the war and about how to write about the war. Recent scholarship has tired of this problem and has tended to study Thucydides' text as if it were the polished product of a single spell of thinking and writing; but, although Thucydides undoubtedly was a man who devoted great care to what he wrote, ignoring the problem may lead to mistaken judgments of his intentions at some points.

Sources of Information

Classical Athenian society was a society in which writing was used for various public and private purposes (probably more so than in some other Greek cities), but it was still a society in which writing was less important and oral communication more important than they have been in our world in recent centuries. In many contexts the natural way to obtain information was not to look at a book (and of course neither newspapers nor websites existed) but to ask somebody who was in a good position to know. That will have been the case with much of the information which Thucydides wanted for his history, and he will have started from what he already knew and have added to that primarily by questioning people. In his chapter on how he set about writing his history he says:

> On the events of the war [in contrast to the speeches, on which see below] I did not think it proper to write on the basis of chance encounters, or of my own judgment [of what is likely to have happened], but of events at which I was present myself and in the other cases investigating each matter with as much accuracy as possible. This proved arduous, since those who were present at each of the events did not give the same accounts of the same matters, but each reported in accordance with his own partiality and memory. (I. 22. ii–iii, cf. VII. 44, 71)

When he was exiled he had access to people on the Peloponnesian side as well as the Athenian (V. 26. v). He is well qualified to write about the plague which afflicted Athens from 430 to 427/6, because he suffered from the disease himself and saw others suffering from it (II. 48. iii).

Some of the information which he wanted will have been available in texts inscribed in public or kept in somebody's records: treaties (and in parts but only parts of his history he directly quotes the texts of some treaties); who commanded a campaign, what forces were sent, what money was spent on them. However, even in those cases he may not always have consulted records, and no records will have stated why a campaign was undertaken, whether it was controversial or what then happened. Documents underlie passages in other parts of his history, but they are directly quoted only in IV. 117–V. 83 and VIII, and there has been discussion of why such quotations occur in those parts of his history only: do they represent an early stage in the composition, to be eliminated when the narrative was given its final form? or do they represent a change in Thucydides' view of the war or of how he ought to write about it?

Herodotus had frequently given alternative versions, sometimes but not always indicating which he preferred and why, and had said that it was his job to report what he had heard but not necessarily to believe it (II. 123. i, VII. 152. iii). Thucydides, having realised the difficulties in getting the facts right but having made the effort to do that, expected readers to believe that he had succeeded: almost always he does not indicate the sources of his information, and it is only very rarely that he reveals the existence of alternative versions or expresses any uncertainty – for instance,

> … otherwise, the Plataeans said, they would kill the men whom they held alive. When the Thebans had withdrawn from their territory, they would return the men to them. This is what the Thebans say, and they claim that the Plataeans confirmed it by an oath; but the Plataeans deny that they promised to return the men immediately, claiming that there were first to be talks to try to reach an agreement, and they say that they did not swear an oath. (II. 5. v–vi).

In I. 138. iv, on the death of Themistocles, he says what he believes and then mentions an alternative. In IV. 122, on whether the city of Scione defected from Athens to Sparta before or after the year's truce of 423 was made, he reports a disagreement and states firmly the correct answer, that it defected after (and therefore was not entitled to do so). In VIII. 87, on why the Persian satrap Tissaphernes did not bring Phoenician ships to the Aegean to support Sparta, he begins with uncertainty but arrives at a conclusion.

It was hard to discover how many men fought in the Spartan army at the battle of Mantinea in 418, because of 'the secrecy of the state', but from the structure of the Spartan army he makes a calculation (V. 68. ii–iii), as he calculated from the Catalogue of Ships in book II of the *Iliad* how many men were in the Greek force which attacked Troy (I. 10. iii–v); and in fact many scholars think that he has omitted one level from the structure of the Spartan army and that the army was larger than he reckons. It is typical of Thucydides that he gives this information about Sparta at the point where it seems most relevant, before a particularly large-scale and important battle, rather than at the beginning of the war. Exceptionally, he here admits to uncertainty about motivation: in the manoeuvres before the actual battle, when king Agis led the Spartan army towards the enemy one man shouted out that he was aiming to cure one error with another, and he withdrew, 'whether because of the shout or because he had some sudden thought whether different or on the same lines' (65. ii–iii).

It is not certain, he states, whether the account finally accepted of Athens' religious scandals in 415, the mutilation of the herms and the profanation of the Eleusinian Mysteries, was correct or not, but the fact that the case was closed was of great benefit to Athens (VI. 60. ii–v). It was even harder to find out what happened in the night-time battle at Syracuse in 413 than to find out what happened in daytime battles (VII. 44. i–ii).

What he reports is intrinsically credible, but we cannot always be sure that he is right. There are not many places where he can be checked against other evidence, but where he can there are problems. For two Athenian squadrons of ships sent to Corcyra in 433 he names the commanders (I. 45. ii, 51. iv), and there survives an inscription recording payment to the commanders from the treasury of the goddess Athena (M&L 61, trans. Fornara 126). For the first squadron the texts agree, but for the second they do not, and the easiest explanation of the disagreement is that Thucydides has made a mistake. He names Glaucon and Andocides; the inscription names Glaucon, Metagenes and Dracontides; and probably Andocides and

Dracontides both had fathers called Leogoras. In Athens' oligarchic revolution of 411 (when Thucydides was in exile, and dependent on what he learned from others) he has preparatory work done by a board of ten men (VIII. 67. i), while other texts report an already-existing board of ten (mentioned by Thucydides earlier: VIII. 1. iii) to which 20 others were added (*Ath. Pol.* 29. ii, cf. Androtion *FGrH* 324 F 43 = Philochorus *FGrH* 328 F 136, trans. Fornara 148), and probably that is right. Nevertheless, given his insistence on establishing the facts correctly, and the inherent credibility of his narrative, we should assume that normally he did succeed.

Selection and Presentation

Thucydides does not report only facts of that kind. He frequently says why states or individuals did what they did, and where a modern writer might cite a source or indicate that this is a conjectural interpretation he reports these matters likewise simply as facts. Sometimes they will be derived from an authoritative source: in IV. 105. i he says that the Spartan Brasidas knew about Thucydides and was in a hurry to win over the city of Amphipolis before Thucydides could arrive and make it harder for him to do so, and it is likely that after he was exiled as a result of this episode he was able to talk to Brasidas or to sombody close to him. At other times they will be guesses, and not necessarily good guesses, as when, in IV. 27. iii–iv and 28. ii, in connection with the affair at Pylos in 425, he attributes discreditable motives to the Athenian Cleon, whom he disliked: Cleon was suspect, Thucydides says, because he had opposed Sparta's peace offer; he was afraid that he would be exposed as having given false information about the situation at Pylos; and he was frightened when he realised that Nicias seriously intended to hand over the command to him.

Thucydides also includes in his history many speeches, often pairs of opposed speeches; and in I. 22. i, before proceeding to the events in his history, he remarks on his speeches, but unfortunately with an ambiguity which has prompted debate ever since. Nowadays, popular writers may allow themselves more latitude, but serious historians would not attribute words to individuals in inverted commas unless it was known that those are the words which the individuals actually used. Thucydides states:

> As for the speeches which men made, either before the war or when it was under way, it was hard for me to make an accurate record of what was said, both of the speeches which I heard myself and of those reported to me from various other places. The speeches here give what I judged it most appropriate for each man to say in the circumstances in question, while keeping as close as possible to the *xympasa gnome* of what was actually said. (I. 22. i)

But how has he held the balance between what he judged appropriate and what was actually said? And does *xympasa gnome* mean simply the overall sense (for instance, in I. 79–87, in Sparta in 432, that Archidamus did not want an immediate war against Athens but Sthenelaïdas did), or is Thucydides claiming more than that?

Throughout his work Thucydides' language makes heavy demands on his readers, and this is particularly true of his comments on events and of his speeches. The condensed and difficult style of the speeches is surely his own, and it is hard to believe that politicians hoping to persuade a mass audience would speak in this way (but they are not totally uniform: Sthenelaïdas in I. 86 is a convincingly curt Spartan, and some recent work suggests that speakers are given distinctive voices, and distinctive effects on their audiences, to a greater extent than has usually been allowed).

In content, a speech delivered in one context may respond to a speech delivered earlier in a different context to an extent which is unlikely to be authentic (though of course some information on what had been said may have reached the later speaker): for instance, in 432/1 Pericles in Athens in I. 140–5 picks up things said in Sparta in I. 67–88, 119–24. The Corinthians say to the Spartans, 'You know both that to the greater extent it was the barbarians who tripped over themselves; and that against the Athenians themselves we have on many occasions so far survived through their own mistakes rather than retribution on your part' (I. 69. v), and Pericles says to the Athenians, 'I am afraid more of our own mistakes than of our opponents' intentions' (I. 144. i). Archidamus says of the Athenians, 'One might perhaps be confident … that we can overrun their land and ravage it. But they have a great deal of other land which they rule, and they will be able to import what they need by sea' (I. 81. i–ii), and Pericles says, 'It will no longer be comparable for even a part of the Peloponnese to be laid waste and the whole of Attica: for they will not be able to take other land in return without fighting, but we have abundant land in the islands and on the mainland; for control of the sea is a great advantage' (I. 143. iv–v).

Speeches to the troops attributed to commanders before battles have aroused particular suspicion among some readers, who have doubted whether speeches of the Thucydidean kind would, or even could, have been made in such a context; and, whatever the practicalities on such occasions, we should at any rate grant that such speeches are less likely to have been well remembered than speeches to an assembly.

In selecting material Thucydides will inevitably have focused on arguments which seemed to him important rather than arguments which seemed to him unimportant, and sometimes the result may give a distorted impression of what had originally been said. The frequent occurrence in speeches of discussions of the nature of Athenian power may reflect Thucydides' interest in the subject rather than its frequency in public debate. In 427 Athens suppressed a revolt by Mytilene, a Delian League member on the island of Lesbos, and its first decision was to execute all the men and enslave all the women and children (III. 36. ii). The next day, Thucydides writes, the Athenians changed their minds, and 'reckoned that it was a savage policy and a drastic decision to destroy a whole city rather than those who were guilty' (36. iv). He then gives a debate in which Cleon, the author of the original decision, defends it and Diodotus argues successfully for a (slightly) less severe punishment (36. v–49). Both speakers focus on what would be to Athens' advantage; Cleon rejects any appeal to pity (37. ii, 38. i, 40. ii–iii); Diodotus in his speech objects to decisions taken in anger (42. i, 44. iv), but nowhere does he say that the original punishment would be cruel: are we to believe that in the actual debate he did not say that?

Nevertheless, Thucydides did hear some speeches (in Athens before he was exiled), and will have been able to find out to some extent what was said in others. The minimal interpretation of *xympasa gnome* represents a degree of authenticity so slight that it would not have been worth claiming, and I believe that, written up in his own way, the speeches contain arguments which actually were used or which he sincerely (though perhaps on occasions mistakenly) believed might have been used.

We have an indication from Rome of the kind of line Thucydides may have followed. The emperor Claudius in A.D. 48 proposed that leading men from Gaul should be admitted to the senate. We do not, of course, have a recording of what he actually said, but we have an inscription giving the official text published afterwards of what he said, and we have a version of the speech in Tacitus' *Annals* (*CIL* xiii 1688 = *ILS* 212 = Smallwood, *Docs.... Gaius* 369; Tac. *Ann.* XI. 24; both translated Lewis and Reinhold[3], 52–5). Tacitus has comprehensively rewritten Claudius' speech, but he still presents Claudius' arguments rather than a totally different speech. To confirm that in that sense the speeches do have a degree of authenticity, it should be noted also that speeches in contemporary tragedies use the same kinds of argumentation as we find in Thucydides' speeches.

The extent to which he allows speakers to disagree with one another, on matters of fact and opinion, warns us that no speech should be read as a direct expression of Thucydides' own views. In the debate on Mytilene in 427 Cleon says, 'Do not pin the blame on the oligarchs and acquit the people; for all alike attacked us, though they could have come over to our side' (III. 39. vi), but Diodotus replies, 'At present the ordinary people in all the cities are well disposed to you, and either refuse to join the oligarchs in rebellion or, if compelled to join them, promptly become enemies of the rebels' (III. 47. ii). In his own narrative Thucydides had written,

> When even Salaethus no longer expected the ships [sent by Sparta to support the rebels], he armed the ordinary people, who previously had been unarmed, intending to attack the Athenians. But when they had received their arms the people were no longer willing to obey their commanders. At informal meetings they insisted that either the ruling class should bring out the food in public and distribute it to all of them or they would themselves make an agreement with the Athenians and hand over the city to them. (III. 27. ii–iii)

Some scholars have seen in that support for Diodotus' claim that the lower classes were pro-Athenian, but others have seen in it only that at that stage the lower classes were starving.

While there are still some ascriptions of opinion in indirect speech, direct speech as used in the rest of the history is absent from book V after the Peace of Nicias, chapters 25 to end (except that in chapters 85–111 we have the Melian dialogue), and from VIII – approximately the sections of the history in which we do have direct quotation of documents (cf. above).

Thucydides has not, of course, and he could not have, chronicled every event which occurred during the war, or even every event which could be considered relevant to the history of the war (on that question cf. below). Only once does he explicitly say that he is being selective: Athens' war in Sicily between 427 and 424 is reported in a number of short passages, low-key apart from the final section, in which a debate among the Sicilian Greeks leads to a treaty in which the Athenians have to acquiesce (first III. 86, finally IV. 58–65). In the third of these passages he writes, 'There were various campaigns in Sicily, both by Greek Sicilians against one another and involving the Athenians and their allies. I shall record the most important actions of the allies with the Athenians or of the other side against the Athenians' (III. 90. i). There is in fact a papyrus fragment, probably from the fifth-century writer Antiochus of Syracuse or a later writer using him, which contains some information on the war in Sicily not given by Thucydides (*PSI* xii 1283 = *FGrH* 577 F 2). As for events in the Greek heartland, we happen to know that the third-century historian Philochorus recorded an Athenian campaign against Euboea in 424/3 of which there is no mention in Thucydides (*FGrH* 328 F 130).

Omission and Inclusion

Sometimes the absence of information seems due not to deliberate choice but to carelessness by Thucydides. In 429 the Athenian general Phormio won two battles against superior numbers of Peloponnesian ships in the Gulf of Corinth (II. 83–92); and in the winter of 429/8, after a campaign in Acarnania, on the west coast of Greece north of the Gulf, Phormio returned to Athens (II. 102–3). In 428 the Athenians sent a fresh squadron of ships round the Peloponnese to the Gulf, 'appointing Asopius son of Phormio as general, since the Acarnanians had urged them to send a son or relative of Phormio as commander' (III. 7. i). Why was Phormio himself no longer available? The fourth-century writer Androtion had a story of Phormio's being sentenced to a fine which he could not pay, but when the Acarnanians wanted him to be sent as general the Athenians resorted to a device to enable him to pay it (*FGrH* 324 F 8, trans. Fornara 130). Probably that belongs to an earlier occasion, and in 428 Phormio was no longer available because he had died. Thucydides ought in any case to have given an explanation: perhaps when he wrote III. 7 he thought he had supplied the information in II. 103, and simply did not check. Another near-silence is hard to make out. The Athenians sent further ships to reinforce those which Phormio had in the Gulf, but they first accepted an invitation to intervene in a dispute in Crete and arrived only after the battles: Thucydides mentions this briefly in II. 85. v–vi, 92. vii. Are we to assume that he was himself critical of this diversion? 'Which ought to have reached Phormio before the naval battle' (92. vii) suggests that he was, but we cannot be sure.

In IV. 50. ii–iii Thucydides steps outside his chronological framework to note that an episode involving the Greeks and Persia ended with an Athenian embassy to Persia which turned back on learning of the death of Artaxerxes I; but he does not mention either there or elsewhere (if it is true: not all accept this) that other evidence suggests that once Darius II was established on the throne the Athenians did make a treaty with him.

There is a possible omission in connection with the battle of Mantinea in 418. For a time the Spartan army was manoeuvring in the southern part of the plain of Tegea and Mantinea, in Arcadia, and the army of Athens, Argos and allies in the northern part. The battle was fought when the Spartans, marching northwards, unexpectedly encountered the enemy, marching southwards, and were so badly positioned that they might well have been defeated, though in the event they were not (V. 62–73). 'The Spartans were the most astounded in this crisis of all the occasions which could be remembered' (66. ii); but how did it come about that they did not realise until the last minute that the enemy were marching towards them? Several scholars, though not all, have thought that this can best be explained if there was a wood in the middle of the plain which blocked the view, though the wood is first mentioned only in the second century A.D. by the traveller Pausanias (VIII. 11. i).

There are some kinds of explanatory matter which a historian may think will be needed by his readers, or by some of them, or else may consider unnecessary. Sometimes Thucydides remembers that he is not writing only for contemporary Athenians, as when he explains Athens' funerals for men killed in battle:

> In the same winter [431/0] the Athenians complied with their traditional law, and held a public funeral of the first men to die in this war, in the following way. First, on the third day before, they set up a tent and lay out in it the bones of the dead, and each man brings to his own the offerings that he wishes. When the procession is held, waggons carry cypress-wood coffins, one for each tribe, with each man's bones in his own tribe's coffin. One empty bier is carried, laid out for the missing, whose bodies could not be found and recovered. Every man who wishes, of the citizens and the foreigners, joins the procession, and the women of the families are present to lament at the grave. So they are placed in the public tomb, which is located in the most beautiful suburb of the city. Those who die in war are always buried there, apart from those who died at Marathon [fighting against the Persians in 490]: the Athenians judged their virtue to be outstanding, and established their tomb on the spot. When they have been covered with earth a man chosen by the city, whose mind is judged not to be lacking in intelligence and whose reputation is outstanding, makes the appropriate speech of praise over them. After this the people depart. (II. 34. ii–vi)

Again, he is thinking of non-Athenian readers when he writes of Acharnae as 'the largest of the places in Attica called demes' (II. 19. ii), and of 'what is called the coastal territory, ... as far as Laurium, where the Athenians have their silver mines' (II. 55. i). But sometimes he does not, and references to Pericles' not summoning an assembly or summoning one (II. 22. i, 59. iii, cf. IV. 118. xiv) have left us uncertain what powers Athenian generals had in that respect.

He has a tendency to give geographical notes on places on the fringes of the Greek world, which presumably were familiar to fewer people (e.g. III. 88, on the Islands of Aeolus, north of Sicily; 92. vi; 105. i), and not on more central places (in IV. 67. v, 'where the trophy now is', and in 69. ii he assumes detailed knowledge of Megara); but his account of a campaign of 426/5 in the north-west of Greece has not made it clear where all of the places which he names were (III. 105–14), and there are notes on places in the Peloponnese which might well have been judged unnecessary, such as 'The land of Thyrea [where Sparta settled the people expelled by Athens from Aegina in 431] is on the borders of Argive and Laconian territory, reaching down to the sea' (II. 27. ii, repeated at IV. 56. ii; another such note is II. 56. v). However, the comment on the location of Decelea in the north of Attica, where the Spartans had a fort in the last years of the war, 'Decelea is about 120 stades [11 miles / 18 km] from the city of Athens, and about the same or not much more from Boeotia' (VII. 19. ii), is more easily justified as important for the narrative.

On other occasions information may have been omitted because the omission suited Thucydides' narrative purpose. Examples of this can be found in his treatment of the events of the late 430s which led to the outbreak of the war. In explaining how the war came about he distinguished 'the truest reason, most concealed in word', Athens' growing power and Sparta's fear of it, from 'grievances and disputes, publicly mentioned', of which he nevertheless proceeds to give what he considers a definitive account, 'so that nobody should ever need to ask' (I. 23. iv–vi). In VI. 6. i he has a 'truest reason' for Athens' Sicilian expedition of 415, a desire to rule Sicily, which he contrasts with a 'respectable-seeming' wish to support Athens' kin and allies.

For the 'grievances and disputes' leading to the war he provides a detailed narrative of two episodes, each of which ended with fighting between Athenian and Corinthian forces, Corinth being a member of Sparta's Peloponnesian League. In 433 Athens made an alliance with Corcyra, off the west coast of northern Greece, a colony of Corinth but on bad terms with it, and supported Corcyra against an attack by Corinth; but the alliance was made purely defensive so that Athens could claim not to be in breach of the peace made with the Peloponnesians in 446/5 (I. 24–55). In 432 Athens attacked Potidaea, in the north-west of the Aegean, colonised by Corinth and still on good terms with it but a tribute-paying member of Athens' Delian League; and Corinth sent troops to support Potidaea, but volunteers rather than an official Corinthian force, so that it could claim not to be in breach of the peace (I. 56–66). Two other 'grievances and disputes' are not treated similarly but are mentioned briefly in the debates which follow: the island state of Aegina claimed that Athens was denying it the autonomy promised in a treaty, about which Thucydides tells us no more (I. 67. ii, 139. i, 140. iii); and Megara, on the isthmus between Athens and Corinth, complained of being subjected to economic sanctions by Athens because of a dispute over sacred land and runaway slaves (I. 67. iv, 139. i, 140. iii, 144. ii).

Yet even Thucydides' narrative indicates that Megara was a particular bone of contention, and other texts confirm that; and in 431, the first year of the war, the Athenians expelled the inhabitants of Aegina, 'complaining that they were not least to blame for the war' (II. 27. i), and began a series of biannual attacks on Megara (II. 31, IV. 66. i). Why is Thucydides' treatment so unbalanced? My own guess is that in the cases of Corcyra and Potidaea Thucydides the Athenian was satisfied that Athens was in the right; on Aegina we have no information on which to base a judgment; the sanctions against Megara were probably against the spirit but not against the letter of the treaty of 446/5, and the fact that others made much of Megara (e.g. the comedian Aristophanes' *Acharnians*, 515–36, 719–835, performed in 425) may have prompted Thucydides to play it down.

In the section on Corcyra Thucydides has a debate in the Athenian assembly, at which envoys from Corcyra and Corinth make speeches (I. 31–43), and he then states that the asssembly met twice (very probably on successive days), and on the first day inclined towards the Corinthians but on the second changed its mind and decided on a defensive alliance with Corcyra (44). Probably Thucydides was present, and even if he was not he could surely have found out: which Athenians were on which side (neither Pericles nor any other Athenian is named)? which, and how many, changed their minds, and why? Probably Pericles was in favour of Corcyra (Plut. *Per.* 29. i says so, but we do not know on what basis), and the fact that one of the commanders of the first Athenian squadron was Cimon's son Lacedaemonius has led me to suspect that he had inherited his father's anti-Periclean and pro-Spartan politics and favoured Corinth, and that his command is a sign that Pericles' opponents, although defeated, were still strong enough to have one of their men appointed. Thucydides believed in an Athens which was firmly and wisely controlled by Pericles (II. 65. v–ix), and it suited him to minimise the signs of opposition and to show Athens as a whole moving towards the unavoidable war (cf. Pericles in I. 140–4). Contrast the much more revealing account of the occasion in 425 when Cleon was forced into taking command of the Athenian operations at Pylos, and Thucydides gives an unfavourable picture of him (IV. 27–8).

After the original squadron of ten ships to Corcyra Athens sent a further squadron of twenty, and Thucydides mentions these when they arrive at Corcyra (I. 50. v). There must have been a further debate in Athens, resulting in the decision to support Corcyra more strongly: does Thucydides suppress that because he does not want to emphasise the change in policy, or is it simply that he does not want to interrupt his narrative of what was happening at Corcyra by switching back to Athens? Similarly, in 427 embassies and fleets from elsewhere are mentioned when they arrive at Corcyra (IV. 69–85): this avoids interruptions to the flow of the narrative, and the various arrivals do affect the situation in Corcyra and prepare the way for the discussion in 82–3 of how the war affected local tensions.

Uncharacteristically, after a double defeat of the Ambraciots in 426/5, Thucydides writes, 'I have not recorded the number of the dead, because the total said to have perished would seem incredible in proportion to the size of the city' (III. 113. vi) – and that may well create a greater impression of enormity than the actual figures would have done (Ambracia was one of the larger Greek cities, but not a very large city). The plague at Athens killed 4,400 hoplites and 300 cavalry, and the number of the rest could not be discovered (III. 87. iv) – and that refusal to give the number of the rest perhaps serves to strengthen our belief that the figures which Thucydides does give are correct. When the Spartans occupied Decelea, in Attica, from 413 onwards, 'more than twenty thousand slaves deserted' (VII. 27. v): how the figure could have been established we cannot tell, but is 'more than twenty thousand' intended to look more precise than 'about twenty thousand'?

On a larger scale, Thucydides' understanding of what should be included in a history of the Peloponnesian War is narrow. Military actions, and the decisions which led to them, are carefully reported, though as we have seen there are occasions when more might have been said about the politics behind the decisions. He believes that what was primarily at issue in the war was the Athenian empire, and his speeches focus frequently on the morality of Athenian power. However, as we shall see in the next chapter, after indicating the main features of the Delian League at its foundation (I. 96–97. i), and remarking in general terms on Athens' severity in insisting on the allies' obligations (I. 98, iv–99), he says very little about how the League functioned and how Athenian power was exercised.

The tribute paid by the allies was important in helping to fund Athens' military activities (I. 80. iii, 81. ii–iii, 83. ii, 122. i, 143. v, II. 13. ii), but he does not give figures except at the foundation of the League and in 431 (I. 96. ii, II. 13. iii), in each case in fact higher than other evidence would suggest (I suspect that they are derived from optimistic assessment lists rather than from records of sums actually received). In the Athenian and Peloponnesian speeches before the outbreak of the war, in book I, he frequently calls attention to the importance of finance and to Athens' superiority in that respect, and at the beginning of the war he attributes to Pericles a review of Athens' resources (II. 13. iii–ix). Afterwards, however, financial considerations do often surface, for instance:

> Since the Athenians were short of money for the siege [of Mytilene in 428/7], they levied an *eisphora* of two hundred talents on themselves for the first time, and they also sent out to the allies to raise money twelve ships under Lysicles and four other generals. (III. 19. i)

(Comparable passages are II. 69. i, IV. 50. i; also VII. 27. ii, 28. iv, VIII. 1. ii.) But we are given just enough information to make us long for more. What does Thucydides mean when he says that the *eisphora* (an *ad hoc* property tax on the rich) of winter 428/7, which raised 200 talents, was levied 'for the first time'? The first ever, or the first in the war, or the first to raise as much as 200 talents? Why did he not think it worth mentioning the decree of 425 to reassess the tribute of the allies at a much higher level, which we know from an inscription (M&L 69, trans. Fornara 136)? Did the harbour tax which replaced the tribute in 413 succeed in raising more money than the tribute, as was hoped (VII. 28. iv)? And did the Athenians continue with that to the end of the war, or did they later, perhaps after the point at which Thucydides' narrative ends, revert to tribute?

Thucydides reveals that to some extent Athens relied on non-Athenians to row the navy's ships (I. 121. iii, 143. i), but nowhere does he indicate what proportion of the oarsmen were non-Athenian. Did the Athenians at first regularly pay sailors 1 drachma per day (III. 71. iv, in a chapter which is perhaps interpolated, VI. 31. iii) but after the disaster in Sicily in 413 reduce the rate to ½ drachma (VIII. 45. ii), or ought these passages to be explained in some other way (1 drachma an exceptional rate on exceptional occasions, or Alcibiades in VIII deceiving the Persian satrap Tissaphernes)? The Peloponnesians in their summer invasions of Attica in the early years of the war ravaged the countryside (notice especially II. 55, III. 26. ii–iii). After the establishment of their fort at Decelea in the north of Attica in 413 they were able to do this all the year round and to do more harm to the Athenians (VII. 27. iii–v); but how much damage was done to Athenian agriculture and the silver mines, in the short term and in the long? A modern expert has reported that, while standing cereals and vegetables could be destroyed in whatever fields the invaders reached on the various occasions, it would have been very difficult to do long-term damage to figs, vines and olives.

On the working of the state's machinery, even for his own Athens, he gives only the information which he considers necessary, and does not indicate what powers the generals had with regard to the convening of the assembly (cf. above), or state directly that the ten generals (the number, cf. I. 116. i) were appointed by election (cf. II. 65. iv), normally one from each of the ten tribes though at the time of the Peloponnesian War some exceptions were possible, and that there were no restrictions on re-election. For 411 (when he was in exile) he does state that under the original oligarchy Athens was ruled by a body of Four Hundred and a larger body of Five Thousand was envisaged but never activated (VIII. 67–70, cf. 65. iii, 72. i, 86. vi, 89. ii–iii, 92. xi, 93. ii); but when 'the Athenians' deposed the Four Hundred and 'voted to entrust affairs to the Five Thousand', he expresses admiration for this regime but does not give any precise information on how it functioned (VIII. 97. i–ii) The democratic council of 500, which prepared the assembly's business and was central to Athens' administration, appears (apart from the preambles of a few quoted documents) only in a story in which Alcibiades tricks Spartan envoys (V. 45. i), and in the oligarchic revolution of 411, when it was still meeting until the final *coup* but after that allowed itself to be paid off for what remained of its year of office (VIII. 66. i, 69–70. i). The equivalent body in Sparta, the *gerousia* (council of elders), he never mentions at all.

Thucydides' attitude to religion we shall look at in the next chapter. Here we must note that, while he does sometimes mention religious matters and religious reasons for action (in 426/5 the Athenians in response to an oracle 'purified' the sacred island of Delos by removing all the bodies buried there, III. 104; for a sequel, and another oracle, see V. 1, 32. i), on other occasions when he might have done so he does not. The men escaping from Plataea in 428/7 'had shoes on the left foot only, to give them a safe grip on the mud' (III. 22. i): presumably two bare feet would have been still safer than one, but one bare foot seems to have been a rite to invoke the support of the gods of the underworld. On one occasion he explicitly rejects a religious explanation: in connection with the battle of Mantinea in 418 he remarks that the Spartan army 'advanced slowly, with many pipers stationed in the ranks in the customary way, not for religious reasons but so that they should march in step with the rhythm and their formation should not be broken' (V. 70).

There are other interesting negatives, not connected with religion. In I. 105. iii–iv, in the early 450s, the Corinthians invaded the Megarid, thinking the Athenians would be unable to support Megara while they had forces committed in Aegina and in Egypt; but the Athenians 'did not disturb the force in Aegina' but sent their oldest and youngest to fight against the Corinthians. Thucydides has attributed a motive to the Corinthians, perhaps correctly. 'Did not disturb' looks innocuously factual; but what are we to see behind it?

that Athens did not react as the Corinthians hoped? as another city might have done? after a debate in which some did want to disturb the force in Aegina?

When the Peloponnesian invasion of Attica in 426 was aborted because of earthquakes, Thucydides gives no further explanation (III. 89. ii), when the reason might have been either or both of a fear of physical danger and a fear that they were a divine warning. Similarly on other occasions when an earthquake leads to a suspension of business or a change in military plans he does not give a reason. He does, however, say that the Spartans believed that the great earthquake which hit Sparta c. 465/4 was punishment for an act of sacrilege against Poseidon (I. 128. i). In his narrative the Spartans are particularly likely to let religious considerations affect their action (e.g. IV. 5. i, V. 54. ii, 75. ii, 82. iii; cf. the Syracusans, VII. 73. ii, and the Corinthians, VIII. 9. i), and the Athenians particularly unlikely (but in VII. 50. iv Nicias allows an eclipse to delay the Athenians' withdrawal from Syracuse in 413). Most of his instances of earthquakes' affecting human action are on the Spartan side, and it seems likely that this reaction to earthquakes was at least in part religious.

In 426 Sparta founded a colony at Heraclea, west of Thermopylae in northern Greece (III. 92-3). Thucydides does mention that the Delphic oracle was consulted (as it often was before the foundation of a colony), but among the possible reasons for the colony he does not mention a Spartan desire (which there may well have been) to increase its influence in the amphictyony, the 'league of neighbours', including particularly the Thessalians and the peoples surrounding them, which played a part in the administration of the sanctuary at Delphi. Also he does not mention that it was appropriate for Sparta to name the colony after Heracles, since its kings were allegedly descended from Heracles, and that two of the three men in charge of the foundation, Leon and Alcidas, had names apropriate to a colony named after Heracles – Leon because of Heracles and the

Nemean lion, Alcidas a name of Heracles – and the name of the third, Damagon, means 'people-leader'.

The assembly which voted to install Athens' oligarchy of the Four Hundred in 411 was held not in the city as usual but just outside, at Colonus, in a sanctuary of Poseidon (VIII. 67. ii). Thucydides does not give any reason for holding the assembly there. One often suggested is that, with the Spartans at Decelea, the poorer citizens who were likely to be most opposed to the oligarchy would, lacking arms, be the least willing to risk going to Colonus. But one other possibility is that, then as later, men serving in the cavalry were particularly sympathetic to oligarchy, and, because the Poseidon worshipped at Colonus was Poseidon Hippios, 'horsy Poseidon', the place would appeal to them. Whatever the oligarchs' motives may have been, in replacing the democracy with their regime they were trying to comply with democratic criteria of respectability, so they must also have had some respectable-seeming reason for convening the assembly there.

It is not clear how far this line of approach should be followed. In an episode in Macedon in 423 'the Macedonians and the mass of the barbarians immediately took fright, as large forces are apt to be terror-stricken for no obvious reason' (IV. 125. i). Is that to be taken at face value (I believe it is), or is Thucydides here being anti-religious and hinting, 'not, as some people might think, plunged into panic by the god Pan'?

The Earlier History of Greece

Thucydides writes about the history of Greece before 435 in parts of book I: 1–23 iii on the growth of power in Greece, to justify his view that the Peloponnesian War was greater than any previous war; 89–118, on the growth of Athens' power after 478, to justify his view that the truest reason for the war was Athens' power and Sparta's fear of it; 126. ii–138, which begins as an explanation of propaganda points made by the two sides in 432/1 but turns into a study of the Spartan Pausanias and the Athenian Themistocles as the two most distinguished Greeks of their time (138. vi) – and in a few passages elsewhere. Here his starting-point was not his own direct and almost-direct knowledge. He may well still have relied primarily on material which reached him orally, but some narrative histories were available. The *Atthis* (Athenian history) of Hellanicus of Lesbos is mentioned (this is the only time another historian is named), when he is criticised for a treatment of the period after 478 as 'brief and not precise in its chronology' (I. 97. ii), a criticism which we may make of Thucydides' own treatment of that period. The account of Greek colonisation in Sicily (VI. 2–5, cf. III. 88. ii) is likely to be derived from a Sicilian writer, Antiochus of Syracuse.

Above all there was Herodotus (though Thucydides never names him). Thucydides' opening chapter, introducing himself and his subject, is clearly an attempt to trump the opening chapter of Herodotus (who claimed that the Persian force which invaded Greece in 480 was larger than any before it, including the Greek force which attacked Troy: Hdt. VII. 20–1). Two statements which Thucydides claims to expose as erroneous in I. 20. iii are statements made by Herodotus (Hdt. VI. 57. v, IX. 53. ii). And we should not forget Homer: to us the *Iliad* and the *Odyssey* contain invented stories about a war against Troy which was part of the Greeks' mythical past but may itself be pure invention, but to the Greeks they were part of their early history. Homer wrote about a great war; Herodotus and Thucydides wrote about their greater wars, and in various ways they can be seen as doing in their idioms what Homer had done in his. Thucydides when writing about the past cites Homer several times in support of his account (I. 3. ii, 5. ii, 9. iv, 10. iii–v; cf. III. 104. iv–vi, a *Homeric Hymn* which he attributes to Homer).

On the past Thucydides cites other kinds of evidence. Present-day customs in more backward areas point to earlier customs in now more advanced areas (I. 5. ii–vi); ancient burials on Delos he believes show that the inhabitants then were Carians, a people living in his time in the south-west corner of Asia Minor (I. 8. i); the physical appearance of Athens and Sparta shows that powerful states do not necessarily have grand buildings, as Athens does but Sparta does not (I. 10. i–iii). Inscriptions are cited in connection with the account of Pausanias (I. 132. ii–iii), and to support details in a polemical account of Athens' sixth-century tyranny, in which he insists that other people are mistaken about the facts (VI. 54. vi–55. ii; but the further inscription in VI. 59. iii does not similarly help to support an argument). But before citing the inscriptions to support his argument about the tyranny he claims that he can give his version more accurately *akoei*, 'from oral sources' (VI. 55. i). The opening chapters are full of such terms as *tekmerion* ('indication', e.g. I. 1. i) and *semeion* ('sign', e.g. I. 6. ii). On the past as on his own time Thucydides has not always succeeded – his uses of Homer seem to us unsophisticated, and the burial practice which he identified as Carian may not have been uniquely Carian – but we should still judge that he was trying to support his points in the right kinds of way.

Modes of Narrative

Thucydides does not have a single narrative mode, in which all events are chronicled on the same level and in the same tone, but some items are recorded in a low-key, matter-of-fact way (such as the fighting in Sicily in 427–424, noted above; and Athens' naval expeditions in 431 and 430, II. 17. iv, 23. ii, 25, 30, 32; 56, 58, while other episodes are given a detailed and exciting treatment. The size of the naval expedition of 430 is stressed in VI. 31. ii–iii, but there Thucydides mentions it for a different reason: in size it was comparable to the force sent to Sicily in 415, but it was a far less ambitious kind of expedition. The treatment of the Sicilian war of 427–424 is in marked contrast to that of 415–413; but probably Thucydides' account of the years 431–421 was polished to almost its present state soon after 421, and the nature of his treatment of the earlier episode reflects a feeling at the time that it was not very important rather than a desire to play it down in contrast to the later episode. A few examples of detailed episodes, earlier than that of 415–413, among many are the history of Athens' neighbour Plataea from 431 until its capitulation to Sparta in 427 (II. 2–6, 71–8, III. 20–4, 53–68); the revolt of Mytilene against Athens and the suppression of it in 428–427 (III. 2–6, 8–18, 25, 27–50); in 429 the naval battles in the Gulf of Corinth, and afterwards a Spartan plan to attack Athens' harbour at the Piraeus, which failed through lack of nerve (II. 83–94); Athens' success against Sparta in 425 at Pylos in Messenia (IV. 2–6, 8–23, 26–41).

Those episodes, as Thucydides narrates them, are indeed exciting episodes, and he seems to have had a particular interest in the kind of technical details which he supplies for the siege of Plataea and the escape of some of the men being besieged (II. 71–8, III. 20–4; for other instances of technical interest see IV. 100, VII. 34. v, 36. ii–iii):

> After this invocation of the gods, [in 429 the Spartan king Archidamus] set the army to prosecuting the war. First they built a stockade round Plataea with the trees which they cut down, so that nobody could come out against them. Then they built up a mound against the city, hoping that with so large a force engaged in the work they would capture it very quickly. They cut down timber from Mount Cithaeron and built it up against the mound on each side, laying it in a lattice-pattern, to serve as a containing wall and prevent the mound from spreading out to a great distance. On it they placed brushwood, stones, and anything else whose addition would help them finish the job. They continued piling it up without interruption for ??? [the manuscripts have 'seventy', but that is too high a number] days and nights, dividing

the work to give the men breaks, so that some were working while others were sleeping and eating. The Spartans' *xenagoi* ['leaders of foreigners'] commanding each city's contingent compelled the men to persevere in the work.

When the Plataeans saw the mound rising, they constructed a wooden wall, and placed this on top of their own city wall where the mound was being raised against it, and they built into it bricks which they tore down from the houses nearby. They used the timber as a framework, so that the structure should not become weak as it grew in height, and in front they put a screen of skins and hides, to protect the workmen and the timber from flaming arrows and keep them safe. The wall was raised up to a great height, and the mound was piled up opposite it no less energetically. (II. 75)

The Plataeans were able to thwart the Spartans' original attack, but the Spartans then built an outer wall to isolate Plataea. In the winter of 428/7 some of the Plataeans attempted to escape by climbing over the Spartans' wall:

> They made ladders equal to the height of the enemy's wall, measuring from the layers of bricks where the side of the wall facing them had not been plastered. Many men counted together, and, although some would get it wrong, most would achieve the correct calculation, especially as they counted several times and were not far away but the wall could easily be seen for their purpose. So in this way they arrived at the measurement for the ladders, by estimating the dimensions from the thickness of the bricks.
>
> The Peloponnesians' wall was built like this. It had two circuits, one against the Plataeans and one in case anybody should attack on the outside from Athens, and the circuits were about 16 feet apart. In this intervening space lodgings were built and were apportioned among the guards, and the lodgings filled the whole space and gave the impression of a single thick wall with battlements on both sides. At intervals of ten battlements there were large towers, of the same thickness as the wall, stretching from the inner face to the outer, so that there was no passage past the towers but men had to go through the middle of them. (III. 20. iii–21. iii)

The episodes selected for detailed treatment are episodes which enable Thucydides to explore broader themes – which he normally does in that way rather than by switching from narrative to discussion (though there are exceptions in his comments on the moral effects of Athens' plague, in II. 53, and in his discussion of *stasis*, civil dissension, in III. 82–3). As Thomas Hobbes expressed it in the introduction to his 1629 translation of Thucydides, 'The narration itself doth secretly instruct the reader, and more effectually than can possibly be done by precept' (in W. Molesworth [ed.], *The English Works of Thomas Hobbes of Malmesbury*, viii [London: Bohn, 1843], xxii).

Plataea was a small city caught up in the conflict between the great powers, and not saved by Athens in spite of their long-standing alliance and Athens' initial support. The coercion of Mytilene in 428–427 exemplified Pericles' policy of keeping a firm hold on the empire (I. 143. v, II. 13. ii, 63), and demonstrated the futility of Sparta's hope that it could support an island state against Athens. The naval battles in the Gulf of Corinth and the collapse of the Peloponnesians' plan to attack the Piraeus in 429 showed how far the Peloponnesians were from being able to stand up to Athens at sea (but it has been noticed that Thucydides is consistently, and perhaps excessively, disparaging in his treatment of the Corinthian navy). The affair of Pylos in 425 was a great Athenian success, but it was due partly to Cleon, whom Thucydides disliked, and it could be seen as an unPericlean attempt to enlarge the empire during the war, so he seems to have exaggerated the element of chance in it – and it appears that in fact Athens' gaining outposts there, and in the following year on Cythera, an island off the coast of Laconia (IV. 53–7), did not harm the Spartans as much as they feared and the Athenians hoped (IV. 55. i, but contrast 41. ii on the harm which Sparta did suffer from Pylos).

But Thucydides could have placed his emphases otherwise. The capture and destruction of Plataea did not have a significant effect on the course of the war, and need not have been given an elaborate treatment. Athens' naval expeditions of 431 and 430 were large-scale and expensive, to the extent that it has been doubted whether Pericles' strategy for Athens was based on avoiding risks and relying on Athens' resources to outlast the Peloponnesians, as Thucydides claims (I. 144. i, II. 13. ii), and more might have been said about their purpose and about what they did. When the Peloponnesians invaded Attica, although the Athenians did not give them the hoplite battle which they wanted, they did in fact use cavalry to harass them (in 431, II. 22. ii), and it is only when he reaches 428 that Thucydides tells us that they did this each year (III. 1. ii). The campaigning in Sicily in the 420s may at first have been modest in size (20 ships, III. 86. i) and in aims, but a further 40 or more ships were sent later (III. 115. iv–v), and by the end the Athenians were ambitious: the Athenian generals who accepted the final treaty were accused of taking bribes 'when it was possible for them to overcome things in Sicily' (IV. 65. iii, cf. already III. 86. iv at the beginning of the campaign).

Later in the history it is surely in order to make a point, about Athens' using all its might in a small case but then overreaching itself, that Thucydides writes at length in what is now book V on Athens' capture and destruction in 416 of Melos, the last Aegean island to hold out against it (V. 84–116 – but he does not bother to state what Melos had done since the Peace of Nicias to provoke Athens), after disposing in just part of one sentence of Sparta's comparable destruction of Hysiae, a town in the Argolid (V. 83. ii), and then devotes books VI–VII almost entirely to Athens' ambitious but controversial Sicilian campaign of 415–413 and its disastrous outcome. (But there is no reason to doubt that, chronologically, Sparta did destroy Hysiae just before Athens destroyed Melos, and Athens did destroy Melos just before sending its great expedition to Sicily.) Athens' destruction of Melos, like Sparta's destruction of Plataea, did not significantly affect the course of the war; the Sicilian section, to heighten its effect, begins with the certainly untrue claim (after Athens' earlier involvement there) that most of the Athenians 'were unaware of the size of the island and the number of the inhabitants both Greek and barbarian' (VI. 1. i).

Much of the narrative, in the extended episodes as well as in the short reports, is presented with various details in a matter-of-fact way, but the effects of this narration can be extremely vivid, as in the account of the escape of men from Plataea in 428/7 (III. 20–4: cf. above), and the hurried journey of the ship from Athens which took to Mytilene the better news of the Athenians' revised decision:

> They immediately sent another trireme in haste, hoping that they would not find the city destroyed because the other trireme had arrived first: it had a lead of about a day and a night. The Mytilenaean envoys provided wine and barley-meal for the ship, and promised great rewards if it should arrive in time. The voyage was undertaken in such haste that while they were rowing the men fed on barley-meal kneaded with wine and oil, and they took it in turns to sleep while the others rowed. By good fortune there was no contrary wind. The previous ship had not travelled with haste on its distasteful business, but this one hurried in the manner indicated, and so the first arrived far enough ahead for Paches to read the decree and to be on the point of doing what had been decided, but then the seond arrived in its wake and prevented the destruction, That is the degree of danger to which Mytilene had come. (III. 49. ii–iv)

The plague in Athens (probably because of the mutation of diseases over the centuries it is not to be identified with any disease known to us now) is described with details both of the symptoms and of its effects on life in the city (II. 47. iii–54):

> The disease began with a strong fever in the head, and reddening and burning heat in the eyes; and internally the throat and tongue became bloody and the breath unnatural and malodorous. After this followed sneezing and hoarseness, and in a short time the affliction descended to the chest and resulted in violent coughing. When it became established in the heart, it convulsed that and produced every kind of

evacuation of bile for which doctors have names, accompanied by great discomfort. (II. 49. ii–iii)

The bodies of the dead and dying were piled on one another, and people at the point of death reeled about the streets and around all the fountains in their craving for water. The sanctuaries in which people were camping [because of the evacuation of the countryside] were filled with corpses, as deaths occurred even there: the disaster was overpowering, and as people did not know what would become of them they took to neglecting the sacred and secular alike. ... No fear of the gods or law of men had any restraining power, since people judged that it made no difference whether one was pious or not since all alike could be seen perishing. Nobody expected to live long enough to have to pay the penalty for his misdeeds: people thought much more that a sentence already decided was hanging over them, and that before it was executed they might reasonably get some enjoyment out of life. (II. 52. ii–iii, 53. iv)

The report of a campaign in north-western Greece in 426/5 involves first a successful ambush of the enemy by the Athenian Demosthenes and then his trapping of a relieving force from Ambracia. A herald sent from the Ambraciots to ask for the bodies of the men killed in the first battle was shocked to find the great pile of arms taken from the men killed in the second battle, and we are given an unparalleled dialogue between the herald and an Athenian before the herald leaves in despair without completing his business (III. 107–114. i). On a somewhat more formal level, in indirect speech, we have an exchange of heralds between Athens and the Boeotians after Athens' defeat at Delium in 424/3 (IV. 97. ii–99).

That double defeat of the Ambraciots 'was indeed the greatest disaster to strike a single Greek city in the same number of days in the course of this war' (III. 113. vi). Thucydides expected the Peloponnesian War to be 'great and more noteworthy than those before it' (I. 1. i), and he judged that 'this was the greatest arousal for the Greeks and for a part of the barbarians, and one might say for most of mankind' (I. 1. ii); at the end of his introduction he dilates on ways in which it surpassed previous wars: never were so many cities captured and destroyed, so many men exiled and killed, such occurrences of earthquakes and eclipses, droughts and famines, and in Athens there was the deadly plague (I. 23. i–iii).

Thucydides often uses superlative expressions in his narrative. The Athenian force which invaded the Megarid in 431 was 'the largest Athenian force ever assembled together' (II. 31. ii). The Athenians killed in Aetolia, north of the Gulf of Corinth, in 426 were 'the very best contingent of men from the city of Athens to die in this war' (III. 98. iv). The outcome of the episode at Pylos in 425 was 'the most unexpected of the occurrences for the Greeks during this war' (IV. 40. i). The army assembled by the Spartans which failed to fight a battle outside Argos in 418 was 'the finest Greek army yet assembled' (V. 60. iii); and the battle of Mantinea afterwards was 'the greatest battle among the Greeks in the longest time, brought about by the greatest cities' (74. i: it was indeed the largest land battle in the Peloponnesian War). The original force sent from Athens to Sicily in 415 was 'the most expensive and magnificent Greek force sailing from one city up to that time' (VI. 31. i); but at the end, in 413, 'this was the greatest upset for a Greek force' (VII. 75. vii), the killing of the men caught in the Athenian force trying to escape from Syracuse was 'the greatest slaughter and less than none in this war' (VII. 85. iv), and in its outcome the campaign was 'the greatest action in this war, and, from what we hear, in Greek history, most glorious for the victors and most miserable for the destroyed [that last phrase is in verse rhythm, to highlight it further]: for in all respects they were totally vanquished, and suffered nothing slight in any respect, but with utter destruction, as the saying goes, they lost army and navy and there is nothing which they did not lose, and few out of many returned home' (VII. 87. v–vi). 'Few out of many' is an expression which Thucydides has used twice before, at the disastrous end of

Athens' Egyptian campaign of the 450s (I. 110. i), and after the second of the Ambraciots' two defeats in 426/5 (III. 112. viii).

Politics and politicians attract superlatives also. The Athenian Themistocles, who is presented as a forerunner of Pericles, 'disclosed most securely his natural strength, and in that regard was more than others exceptionally worthy of admiration. ... He was the strongest at understanding the immediate situation with a minimum of deliberation, and the best at estimating over the greatest extent what was likely to happen in the future. ... He was best at foreseeing the better and the worse in what was still not evident. To sum up, in the power of his nature and the brevity of his practising he was the strongest at improvising what was needed' (I. 138. iii). And the Spartan Pausanias and Themistocles together were 'the most distinguished of the Greeks of their time' (I. 138. vi). Cleon was 'most violent and most persuasive' (III. 36. vi), and again 'most persuasive' (IV. 21. iii). The later demagogue Hyperbolus escapes superlatives, but was 'a wretched man, ostracised not because of fear of his power and worth but because of his villainy and being a disgrace to the city' (VIII. 73. iii). Nicias, whose portrayal is by no means flattering (as a man afraid of failure rather than eager for success), and whose misjudgments were to a considerable extent responsible for Athens' failure in Sicily in 413, nevertheless when he was caught and killed was 'least deserving of the Greeks of my time to come to such a level of misfortune' (VII. 86. v). Alcibiades, when for once he displayed a Periclean virtue and restrained the Athenian democrats at Samos from leaving their position to intervene in Athens, performed his greatest service for Athens (VIII. 86. iv). Without an actual superlative, 'the Chians to my knowledge alone after the Spartans combined prosperity and prudence, and the more their city advanced and became greater the more securely well-ordered they became' (VIII. 24. iv), while Athens' intermediate regime of 411/10, after the oligarchy of the Four Hundred, was the best in Thucydides' time (VIII. 97. ii).

In recent decades studies of 'narratology', narrative techniques and the effects which they are used to produce, have been profitably applied to Thucydides and have increased our understanding of his artistry. For instance there is 'focalisation', reporting with reference to the eyes through which what is reported is viewed. In V. 31. vi Thucydides explicitly states that the Boeotians and Megarians in 421 avoided joining an Argive alliance 'because, since they were oligarchic, they thought the democracy of Argos would be less suitable for them than the Spartan regime'. In VI. 64. i the Athenian generals wanted to entice the Syracusan army away from Syracuse before they attempted a landing, for otherwise the Syracusan cavalry would harm them, and here although Thucydides does not explicitly say 'they thought' that is clearly what he implies. But what are we to make of III. 49. iv: in 427 the ship taking the news of Athens' first, harsh decision about Mytilene 'had not travelled with haste on its distasteful business': is the business judged distasteful by the sailors or by Thucydides or by both? In IV. 23. i Spartan breaches of their truce with the Athenians at Pylos were 'apparently unimportant' and the Athenians' response was 'wrongdoing' – in whose eyes? Is this simply how the Spartans argued that their technical infringements should not have been held against them, or is Thucydides agreeing with them and therefore criticising the Athenians?

In some passages we are given alternating viewpoints. In III. 93–4, on the Peloponnesians' aborted attack on the Piraeus in 429/8, Thucydides switches between the Peloponnesians' and the Athenians' points of view. In III. 95–101, when the Thracian Sitalces invades Macedon, the route is perceived by the invaders, but in 100–1 the impact of the invasion is perceived by the victims.

Changes of tone can create an effect. In the generally rapid narrative of the period between the Persian Wars and the Peloponnnesian War, after two Athenian victories over the Corinthians (I. 105. v–vi), Thucydides pauses to tell us how some of the Corinthian survivors from the second battle were trapped in an enclosed area from which there was no escape, and the Athenians stoned them all to death; 'and this was a great misfortune for the Corinthians' (I. 106). In 427, when the Spartans finally captured Plataea and killed all the men still there, Thucydides ends the section, 'And the episode concerning Plataea, in the ninety-third year after the Plataeans became allies of Athens, ended in this way' (III. 68. v), and that does not simply round off the section with a chronological fact but adds to the emotional impact of Plataea's being destroyed in spite of its long alliance with Athens.

Rhetorical questions are used only twice. With reference to the night battle outside Syracuse in 413, it is hard enough to establish what happened by daylight, and who could know what happened in a night battle (VII. 44. i)? In 411 after the Spartans won a naval battle against Athens in the Euripus, the strait between Euboea and Athens, and Euboea (which was important to them while the Spartans based on Decelea excuded them from their own countryside) was then lost to the Athenians, how could it not be reasonable that the Athenians should be despondent (VIII. 96. ii)?

Another device to heighten the significance of what did happen is a mention of what almost happened but did not: when the news of Athens' less harsh sentence reached Mytilene just in time, 'that is the degree of danger to which Mytilene had come' (III. 49. iv); and in 414 when Syracuse was considering surrender to the Athenians but the Spartan Gylippus arrived just in time to stiffen the resistance, 'that is the degree of danger to which Syracuse had come' (VII. 2. iv). On a lower level, but still significant, when in 412/11 Athenian and Spartan naval squadrons were anchored on the two sides of a promontory without knowing it, and in response to a message the Spartans departed, 'that is how close Astyochus came to falling into the hands of the Athenians' (VIII. 33. ii–iii). In a cluster of counter-factual suppositions, Sparta might have won the war in 411 if Alcibiades had not prevented the Athenians at Samos from sailing back to Athens

(VIII. 86. iv–v), or if Tissaphernes had brought Phoenician ships into the Aegean (87. iv), or if the Spartans had turned to an attack on Athens after their naval victory in the Euripus (96).

Thucydides was evidently a careful writer who thought about what he wrote and how he expressed it; but, as I noted above, his work was produced over a long period and was not completed or finally polished; and he was working in circumstances in which it was much harder than it is for us today to check when writing one passage what one had written in other passages. So I suggested above that in III. 7. i, when the Acarnanians ask Athens to send a relative of Phormio but Thucydides does not say why Phormio himself was no longer available, the reason may be that he thought he had mentioned Phormio's death in II. 103. i and did not check.

There are many points where we can notice an interesting effect, and have to ask ourselves, and judge the probability for ourselves, whether this is something which Thucydides consciously intended. In the battle outside Amphipolis in 422, in which the Athenian Cleon and the Spartan Brasidas were both killed, the details that Cleon was killed by a barbarian light-armed soldier (V. 10. ix) and that Brasidas was afterwards venerated as a hero (V. 11. i) surely are included to add to the shame of Cleon and the glory of Brasidas.

However, while we must certainly be aware of the possibilities, we must also be wary of over-interpretation. In I. 24. i, after his general statement on the causes of the Peloponnesian War, Thucydides begins his narrative of the period leading to the war, 'Epidamnus is a city ... ', without using a particle, one of the words commonly used in Greek to link a sentence to the preceding sentence. In Hom. *Il.* VI. 152 a section similarly begins, 'There is a city Ephyre ...', without a particle. Is Thucydides consciously echoing Homer, or unconsciously echoing Homer, or simply beginning a new section in a natural way? In II. 63. ii Pericles says that the Athenians 'possess the empire like a tyranny', and in III. 37. ii Cleon says that they 'possess an empire which is a tyranny'. Thucydides surely was conscious that he attributed a remark on the empire and tyranny to both; but is he attributing the same attitude to both, or is he deliberately making Cleon slightly more brutal than Pericles? It is Pericles who goes on to say, 'Though it may be considered unjust to acquire it, to renounce it would be dangerous'.

While Thucydides reports each of the Peloponnesians' invasions of Attica in the early years of the war in its place, he mentions Athens' biannual invasions of the Megarid on the first occasion, in late summer 431, when he states that this happened every year (II. 31), but then not until the last occasion, in late summer 424, and it is only on this occasion that he states that the Athenians invaded twice each year (IV. 66. i). There are various other matters on which Thucydides gives some information at the first mention and further information later. Is this a deliberate 'technique of increasing precision', or does he more simply say at each point what seems to him worth saying there? In the affair of Corcyra and Corinth in 433 the Corinthians are made to say that when Athens was fighting against Samos in 440–439 they by voting against the proposal prevented the Peloponnesian League from going to support Samos (I. 40. v cf. 41. ii). In the fairly detailed narrative of that episode there is no mention of this (I. 115. ii–117); and there are other instances of a point's being mentioned but not where we should most expect it. Is Thucydides deliberately hiding something which would not support the impression which he wishes to make, as politicians today are often accused of 'burying' bad news by releasing it at a time when other matters will attract more attention, or does he (in the case of Samos) simply omit the point from his narrative of the episode because he remembers that he has mentioned it already? If the intention was to lessen the impression that Sparta was already belligerent before the war, he does the opposite when he tells us only in 428, at the time of Mytilene's revolt against Athens, that 'they had wanted to do this even before the war, but had not been supported by Sparta' (III. 2. i).

Overall, as a historian Thucydides claims and we should accept that he tried hard to establish the facts correctly; and he clearly set about it intelligently, though he was not infallible, and there are a few places where we have reason to think that his details are wrong. On the larger scale, he has achieved a masterpiece of putting together what happened and making sense in rational terms of how and why it happened. Again, we are only admitting that he was human when we say that he had his prejudices (about which more will be said in the next chapter), and that he seems to have been too uninterested in some kinds of explanation, such as the religious. His conception of what was required in a history of the Peloponnesian War was narrower than we might wish, but because he has been admired so much that conception has been greatly influential on the subsquent writing of 'serious' history.

3

Thucydides the Thinker

Thucydides did not just report what had happened in the Peloponnesian War, but sought to explain how and why it had happened and what its significance was. However, in common with other earlier Greek writers, he normally did this through his manner of presenting the material and his choice of episodes for detailed treatment rather than by incorporating separate sections of general discussion: in this respect, the discussions which he attaches to the plague in Athens (II. 53) and to the beginning of the civil war in Corcyra in 427 (III. 82–3; 84 is probably an interpolation) are exceptional. This is how his discussion of civil war begins:

> That is how savage the course of the civil war became, and it seemed even worse because it was the first of all. Later indeed one might say that the whole Greek world was turned upside-down, as disputes in each place prompted the democratic leaders to call in the Athenians and the oligarchs to call in the Spartans. In peace they would not have had the excuse or the willingness to invite them; but when they were at war, and there was an alliance available to each side to harm their opponents and at the same time to reinforce themselves, it was easy for those who wanted to bring about a revolution to call in outsiders. Many grave sufferings attacked the cities through civil war, of the kind that continue to happen and always will happen as long as human nature remains the same, but more or less severe, and varying in form, as imposed by the changes of circumstances in individual cases. In peace and favourable conditions both cities and individuals pursue better policies because they are not caught by unwanted constraints; but war, which takes away the ready supply of one's daily needs, and

brings the passions of the majority to the same level as their circumstances, is a violent teacher. (III. 82. i–ii)

On a smaller scale, he uses an ascription of motive to Demosthenes, when he arrived in Sicily with Athenian reinforcements in 413, to comment on Nicias' mismanagement of the campaign (by the end of the year Demosthenes was dead, so Thucydides will not have been able to ask him about his thoughts):

> Demosthenes saw how things were, and thought that he could not waste time and suffer what Nicias had suffered – for when Nicias first arrived he was an object of fear; but because he did not press on Syracuse immediately but wintered in Catana he came to be despised, and Gylippus stole a march on him by arriving with reinforcements from the Peloponnese. But the Syracusans would not even have sent for these if Nicias had attacked immediately, since they thought that they were sufficient, and would not have realised that they were inferior until they were walled off, so that the force would not have helped them so much even if they had then sent for it. (VII. 42. iii)

In the late nineteenth and early twentieth centuries Thucydides tended to be seen as a supremely rational and dispassionate seeker after truth, to an extent which it is now hard to credit (cf. Ch. 4). He was, after all, not an uninvolved outsider but very much an insider, an Athenian from one of the city's leading families, a man who served as a general and who was exiled for his failure to achieve what was expected of him. His report of his involvement in that episode is low-key, and does not indicate why he was at Thasos when he was needed at Amphipolis and Eïon, or enable us to judge whether he was at fault (IV. 104. iv–105). He was also formed intellectually by his context, living in a world in which the stories told by the poets were believed to be stories about the Greeks' actual past history; in which there were stories about gods who intervened in human affairs and themselves behaved and misbehaved like human beings; but in which Herodotus wrote a history which in its range and its intellectual grasp represented a great advance on previous histories, and in which thinkers were questioning the stories about the gods and the nature and very existence of gods, and the bases for right conduct by individuals and by communities. So we should accept that Thucydides did far more than simply report what happened, and that his political and intellectual background will have led him to interpret his material in distinctive ways, with which people from other backgrounds might disagree.

Political Views

Politically it is easy to locate Thucydides in the spectrum but hard to attach a label to him. Over some centuries the Greek cities had developed forms of constitutional government, in which political power was shared among the (adult male) citizens, however they were defined, and which could be contrasted with the rule of a near-eastern monarch or a 'tyrant' who usurped power: the Thebans in III. 62. iii–v describe their regime at the time of the Persian Wars as 'neither an oligarchy based on fair laws nor a democracy, but … what is most directly opposed to laws and the greatest restraint and is closest to tyranny, a clique (*dynasteia*) of a few men'. About the time when Thucydides was born (c. 460) Athens, whose strong navy made the poorer citizens who rowed in it more valuable members of the community than they would have been elsewhere, had gone further in involving the poorer citizens in the running of the state. A distinction between democracies and oligarchies had emerged, and while some Greeks approved of democracy others preferred 'oligarchy based on fair laws', in which more power was given to those who were thought for one reason or another to be more deserving of it. Athens encouraged but did not systematically require democracy among its allies, and Sparta (where there was a measure of political equality among the citizens but they were a small minority within the total population) encouraged oligarchy, and in the second half of the fifth century the polarisation of the Greek world between Sparta and Athens tended to be linked to a polarisation between oligarchy and democracy (cf. III. 82. i, quoted above).

In Athens in the middle of the fifth century Thucydides' relatives Cimon and the elder Thucydides opposed Pericles and the democrats. Thucydides the historian disliked upstart populist politicians such as Cleon (esp. III. 36. vi, IV. 21. iii, 28. v) and Hyperbolus (VIII. 73. iii). When in 425 Cleon was trapped into taking over the command against the Spartans at Pylos, and undertook within 20 days either to bring them to Athens or to kill them there, Thucydides allows himself the amazing comment:

> The Athenians reacted with some laughter to his vain talk; but it was received with pleasure by the people who were sensible, who reckoned that they would achieve one of two good outcomes, either that they would be rid of Cleon, which they thought would be more likely, or that if their judgment was mistaken they would get the better of the Spartans. (IV. 28. v)

Hyperbolus' ostracism is mentioned not at the point when it occurred (417 or 416 or 415: scholars have not been able to agree on the precise year, but I believe 415), but when he was assassinated, in 411, and the indefinite adjective *tis*, 'a certain' Hyperbolus, perhaps adds to the impression of Thucydides' contempt for him.

On the other hand, Thucydides was surprisingly favourable in his final assessment of Nicias (VII. 86. v, cf. what Nicias says of himself in 77. ii), another upstart but one who had behaved in ways acceptable to the old ruling class, and whom he regarded in spite of his failings as a good man; and he was ambivalent over the rogue aristocrat Alcibiades as the Athenians in general seem to have been (cf. Aristophanes' *Frogs*, 1422–36): Alcibiades' greatest service was when like Pericles he restrained the people (VIII. 86. iv). Thucydides disliked the inconstancy of the democratic assembly (e.g. II. 65. iv, IV. 21. iii, VI. 24, 60); he approved of the intermediate regime which followed the oligarchy of the Four Hundred in 411 (VIII. 97. ii), and outside Athens he approved of the 'prosperity and prudence' of Sparta and Chios (VIII. 24. iv).

Nevertheless he clearly admired Pericles, a democratic leader but from the old ruling class, introducing him before his first speech as 'first of the Athenians, most capable both of speech and of action' (I. 139. iv), and giving an enthusiastic final verdict on him as a man who championed wise policies and led the people with a well-judged combination of restraint and encouragement, so that what was 'in theory democracy' was 'in fact rule by the first man' (II. 65. v–x; cf. what Pericles is made to say of himself in II. 60. v–vii). Themistocles, presented as a forerunner of Pericles, and in fact if not positively a democrat an associate of men who later emerged as democrats, is similarly praised for his abilities (I. 138. iii), though since he ended his life in exile he cannot similarly be said to have presided over Athens successfully. In approving of Pericles Thucydides was breaking away from his family background and from his general political attitude. He exaggerated the extent to which one leader, however great, could control the democratically structured Athens; he exaggerated the difference between an unchallenged Pericles and the competing politicians who followed him; and in his disapproval of the risks run by Athens afterwards he made Pericles' strategy for the war seem more defensive and aimed simply at survival in the long term than it may in reality have been.

Right Conduct

How did Thucydides judge the conduct of states and of individuals? One of the contrasts explored by the sophists of the late fifth century was between *physis*, 'nature', which could not be other than it is, and *nomos*, commonly 'law', and in this contrast human convention, what some people in some context have decided one way but other people in another context could decide differently. If laws are not ordained by the gods, what are the basis and the justification for them? Are they, though a human convention, one which is needed to enable human societies to function (as was argued by Protagoras), or are they, as a mere human convention, undesirable, either because they are simply the rules which the strong get away with imposing on the weak (Thrasymachus in Plato's *Republic*) or because they result from a conspiracy among the weak to prevent the strong from living as they otherwise could (Callicles in Plato's *Gorgias*)?

On the level of individual conduct it is clear that, although Thucydides will not have believed that laws came from the gods (I discuss his attitude to religion below), he thought that behaving well and in accordance with the laws was better than behaving badly and contrary to the laws. In discussing the effects of the plague at Athens he remarks with evident disapproval that 'the plague marked the beginning of a decline to greater lawlessness in the city. ... No fear of the gods or law of men had any restraining power. ... No one expected to live long enough to have to pay the penalty for his misdeeds' (II. 53: cf. above). There is similar disapproval in the general comments prompted by the civil war in Corcyra: associations with collaborators

> were formed not with the support of the established laws but for self-seeking in defiance of convention, and the members' pledges of loyalty to one another were reinforced not by divine law but by partnership in lawlessness. ... Most people would rather be called adroit when evil than stupid when virtuous. ... The cause of all this was a desire for power fed by greed and ambition. ... Neither side paid attention to considerations of piety, but if men could cover an objectionable act with fine words it enhanced their reputation. ... Thus civil war brought every form of wickedness to the Greek world, and simple

goodness, which is a major constituent of nobility, was driven by mockery into non-existence. (III. 82–3)

In connection with Athens' religious scandals of 415 he writes that 'the Athenians arrested and imprisoned many positively good men among the citizens through their trust in wretched persons' (VI. 53. ii). Are 'good' and 'wretched' here used simply in a moral sense, or is that combined with a judgment of the social standing of the men in question?

What did Thucydides make of the Athenian empire? His admiration for Pericles seems to include admiration for Athens' imperial achievement under Pericles: 'Under his guidance Athens had risen to its greatest height. Moreover it is clear that, when the war came, he foresaw the strong position that Athens would have in it' (II. 65. v). And so wonderful was the city of Athens that, if it was destroyed, 'one would estimate from the visible appearance of the city that its power was twice as great as it actually is' (I. 10. ii). Surely Thucydides the Athenian was proud of the glorious city of Athens and of its power in the Greek world. Or can we be sure of that? The nature of and the justification for Athenian power is a theme which pervades the whole of his history.

Sparta's final demand to Athens before the war broke out was, he says, 'The Spartans want peace to prevail, and it would if you left the Greeks autonomous' (I. 139. iii); and when the war did break out 'a large majority of people showed the greater good will towards the Spartans, especially because they proclaimed that they were going to liberate Greece' (II. 8. iv). In 432 the Corinthians, urging Sparta to take action before it is too late, paint a picture of an expansionist Athens which has designs on the whole of Greece (I. 68–71), and in a later speech they describe Athens as a tyrant (I. 122. iii, 124. iii). Athenians in Sparta on the first occasion make a speech in which they say Athens deserves its position, has been led to it by considerations of fear, honour and advantage, and ought to be praised for behaving less ruthlessly than its power would allow (I. 73–8), and Athenians later are happy to apply the term tyrant to Athens (Pericles, II. 63. ii; Cleon, III. 37. ii; Euphemus, VI. 85. i).

Thucydides' own narrative notes how Athens' exacting leadership of the Delian League weakened the allies (I. 98. iv–99), and the Mytilenaeans at Olympia in 428 give a subject's-eye view of the growth of Athenian power (III. 10. ii–12). Cleon and Diodotus in 427 discuss how to deal with the defeated Mytilene in terms of Athens' interests (III. 37–48). Euphemus in Camarina in 415/14 again justifies Athenian power, and claims that the Sicilian Greeks need not fear it since in Sicily it is in Athens' interests that the opponents of Syracuse should be strong (VI. 82–7). Most drastically, but not inconsistently with what is said elsewhere, the Athenians in a dialogue with the authorities of Melos, before the city is besieged and captured (this is one of the occasions when it is harder to believe that Thucydides could have obtained a report of what was actually said), say, 'We know and you know that in human discourse considerations of justice apply in cases of equal force, but the strong do what they can and the weak give way. ... We are here for the advantage of our empire' (VI. 84–113, quoting 89, 91. ii).

This has given rise to a series of questions. Can we believe that the Athenians spoke about their empire, among themselves and to others, in that way? Unless Thucydides has been seriously dishonest, the answer must be yes, at any rate sometimes. Is Thucydides right to suggest that, just as it was natural for the Athenians to exercise their power, it was natural for their subjects to hate it (e.g. I. 77. ii–v, II. 63. i, 64. v, III. 10. ii–11, in speeches; cf. the narrative in I. 98. iv–99)? Some scholars have claimed that, while upper-class oligarchs had reason to hate the empire, lower-class citizens of the allied states gained more than they lost; but Greeks did have a strong desire to maintain the freedom of their own communities, and, while democratic political leaders might be conscious that their strong position in their cities depended on Athenian backing, I think on this point Thucydides is closer than his critics to the truth.

Most importantly, for this chapter, what did Thucydides himself think of power exercised in this way and in this spirit? For individuals in their cities Thucydides did believe in obedience to the laws. But there was no formal international law, although it was possible to speak of 'laws of the Greeks' (e.g. I. 41. i), and there were no international courts, although it was possible for states which were at variance to submit to arbitration (e.g. the proposals, in each case rejected by the other side, in I. 28. ii, 78. iv). Was it perfectly acceptable for Athens to exercise its power as far as it could, seeing no third way between the 'freedom' to make others obey it and the 'slavery' of being made to obey others (a frequent *motif*, in Thucydides and elsewhere: e.g. Pericles in II. 63), or was that 'a desire for power fed by greed and ambition', lawlessness on the largest scale? I suspect that Thucydides, the Athenian and the thinker, was torn between pride in the unprecedented achievement of Athens in his time and the feeling that it had been gained by conduct not at all worthy of praise, and that he returned to the subject in his history so often precisely because he could not resolve the dilemma for himself.

Religion

In the field of religion, philosophers such as Xenophanes and Heraclitus had complained that men fashion gods in their own image, and Protagoras had said that it is impossible to know whether gods exist or what they are like. The Athenian Critias at the end of the fifth century wrote a play in which one character said that first laws were invented to control people's behaviour, and then gods were invented to prevent people from breaking the laws when they thought they could escape detection. In Thucydides' time, in Athens and among the Greeks more generally, there is likely to have been a spectrum from those who believed very much as their forebears had believed a century or more earlier to those who had very little belief; but festivals were community or family occasions as well as religious occasions, and it is likely that few if any people openly defied the traditional religion. For Herodotus explanations of events in terms of a divine plan added an extra dimension to explanations in human terms (e.g. Hdt. VII. 1–19 on Xerxes' reasons for invading Greece in 480). The gorge in Thessaly through which the River Peneus flows from the interior to the sea was certainly the result of an earthquake, and can be attributed to the god Poseidon if earthquakes are due to him (Hdt. VII. 129. iv); yet, in more traditional mode, when Persians at Potidaea were caught by an exceptionally high tide after an exceptionally low tide,

> the Potidaeans' explanation of the low tide, the high tide and the Persians' disaster is that these very Persians who were destroyed by the sea had committed sacrilege against the temple and image of Poseidon in the outer city, and I think that in giving this explanation they are speaking well. (Hdt. VIII. 129. iii)

Herodotus did not deny the existence of the anthropomorphic gods; he certainly believed in a divine power which punished impiety, was jealous of excessive human success and had plans for human affairs which were fulfilled in the end; and he believed that the gods spoke to human beings through oracles.

We saw in the previous chapter that Thucydides sometimes, though not systematically, omits religious material and religious explanations when he might have included them. And there is hardly any sign in his history that he himself had any religious belief. There is no divine plan, and events are regularly explained in human terms. Beyond what can be attributed to human decisions, and can therefore be explained and predicted, he refers only to *tyche*, unpredictable 'fortune', as a factor which can be involved in what 'happens' (*xymbainein*). 'By *tyche*' there was no contrary wind, to slow down the ship taking the better news from Athens to Mytilene in 427 (III. 49. iv); and 'by *tyche*' a storm forced an Athenian fleet to pause at Pylos in 425 (IV. 3. i). In 424 the Spartans' morale suffered when 'the many blows of *tyche* which had fallen on them in a short time, contrary to rational expectation, created in them the greatest consternation' (IV. 59. iii). Similar views are attributed to several speakers. 'We are accustomed to blame *tyche* for what happens (*xymbainein*) contrary to rational expectation' (Pericles, I. 140. i). 'Happenings (*xymbainein*) which are sudden, unforeseen and contrary to all rational expectations enslave the spirit' (Pericles on Athens' plague, II. 61. iii). 'It happened (*xymbainein*) that we had considerable adverse *tyche* ... . We must admit that men are sometimes caught out by *tyche*' (Peloponnesian commanders in the Gulf of Corinth, II. 87. ii–iii). 'I think ... I should not in foolish ambition suppose that I am in control equally of my own judgment and of *tyche* which is outside my power' (Hermocrates of Syracuse, IV. 64. i).

In Pericles' speech at the funeral of the Athenians killed in the first year of the war festivals are referred to in secular terms as 'relaxations from toil for the spirit' (II. 38. i), which may reflect Pericles' attitude or Thucydides' or both. When the plague struck Athens religious remedies were as ineffective as the skills of the doctors (II. 47. iv), and as the pious and the impious were afflicted alike no 'fear of the gods or law of men' restrained people from behaving badly if they thought they could get away with it (II. 53. iv). When in his last speech Pericles says with reference to the plague, 'We must bear *daimonia*, "things from the gods", with resignation and blows from the enemy with manliness' (II. 64. ii), that need not mean that he or Thucydides or both seriously believed that the plague had been sent by the gods, any more than English-speakers might if they described it as a 'blow from heaven': we must remember how Pericles referred to the plague earlier in the same speech, as quoted above. Similarly, when Thucydides writes in his narrative of consulting an oracle, 'They sent to Delphi and enquired of the God. ... He responded ... ' (e.g. I. 25. i–ii), this is the language regularly used in such a context and is not a serious indication that Thucydides thought that the God (Apollo) received the enquiry and responded to it.

Thucydides mentions, and sometimes quotes, oracles when he considers them relevant. With reference to Athens' plague he mentions one which referred to a Dorian war (most of Athens' Peloponnesian opponents belonged to the Dorian strand of the Greek people) and with it either a *loimos*, 'plague', or a *limos*, 'famine', and he comments that this time the version with *loimos* was naturally preferred (II. 54. ii–iii). At the beginning of the war, when the Athenians evacuated the countryside of Attica, some of the refugees occupied an area below the acropolis called the *Pelargikon*. An oracle had said, 'The *Pelargikon* is better left alone'; and Thucydides was prepared to accept that, not as a statement from foreknowledge that if the *Pelargikon* were occupied disaster would follow, but simply as a warning that the *Pelargikon* would not be occupied unless Athens were in dire straits (II. 17. i–ii). Later he says there was just one instance of an oracle which gave a correct prediction, the oracle which prophesied that the Peloponnesian War would last 'thrice nine years' (V. 26. iii–iv). However, he writes contemptuously of low-grade oracle-mongers (II. 8. ii, 21. iii, VIII. 1. i).

Natural phenomena are for Thucydides simply natural phenomena, with no further significance. Eclipses are mentioned, and in II. 28 he notes that eclipses of the sun happen only at the new moon. Similarly he notes that an eclipse of the moon in 413 coincided with the full moon, and when Nicias as an Athenian general consulted seers and delayed the withdrawal from Syracuse Thucydides comments that 'he was too much inclined to divination and the like' (VII. 50. iv).

We noticed above that, when earthquakes affect men's actions, Thucydides does not say whether this is for pragmatic or for religious reasons. When earthquakes and a *tsunami* occurred in 426, he explains that the *tsunami* was caused by earthquakes (III. 89. ii–v). In 415/14, at the beginning of the Sicilian campaign, when the Athenians were optimistic, 'there happened (*xymbainein*)' to be a thunderstorm during a battle, and 'for those who were fighting for the first time and had least acquaintance with war this contributed to their fear, but by those who were experienced this was judged to result from the time of year' (VI. 70. i). However, in 413 when the Athenians were withdrawing from Syracuse, it was harder for them to remain rational, and when thunderstorms 'occurred by chance' (Thucydides uses the verb cognate with *tyche*) he first remarks that they tended to occur in the autumn but goes on to say that the retreating Athenians thought all these things were occurring for their destruction (VII. 79. iii).

In 427/6, as part of the war in Sicily, Thucydides reports an Athenian campaign against the Islands of Aeolus (the Lipari Islands, north of Sicily), and he remarks that 'the people there believe that Hephaestus works bronze on Hiera, because a great flame can be seen rising from there by night and smoke by day' (III. 88. iii). He does not say that he believes this himself, and it is not clear why he mentions it: he later refers to eruptions of Etna, on Sicily, simply as a fact of nature (III. 116. i–ii).

Slightly different is the end of Thucydides' introductory section, on the greatness of the Peloponnesian War. What he says first is wholly rational, focusing on disasters attributable to the war: 'It happened that during it there were disasters for Greece such as had not happened in a comparable stretch of time. There had not been so many cities captured and depopulated, in some cases by barbarians and in others by the two sides fighting against one another (and some cities after they had been taken suffered a change of inhabitants); nor so many people exiled and slaughtered, either in the actual course of the war or through dissension (I. 23. i–ii). But he continues: 'What was previously reported by hearsay but more rarely confirmed in fact became not unbelievable: with regard to earthquakes, which attacked over the greatest extent of territory and with the greatest violence; and eclipses of the sun, which occurred with greater frequency than was remembered from earlier time; great droughts in some places and famines resulting from them; and, what caused not the least harm and to some extent death, the disease of the plague. All these things attacked together in conjunction with this war' (23. iii). (Similarly, in Britain at the end of the First World War, Adventists pointed to natural phenomena, including the increase in storms, earthquakes and volcanic eruptions, as signs of the second coming of Christ.) In a comparable spirit, shortly before the outbreak of the war there was an earthquake on Delos (Hdt. VI. 98. i–iii reports an earlier earthquake, and it has been suggested that neither actually occurred but both are based on the misinterpretation of an oracle): he comments, 'It was said, and was believed, that this was significant for what was going to happen' (II. 8. iii). Strictly he is not committing himself to the view that the extremes of nature were increased to match this extreme human conflict. But why should a rational historian choose to mention these extremes at all? Has he simply let his pen run away with itself in these rhetorical flourishes, or does he perhaps wonder if there may be some truth in it after all?

There are at any rate signs that Thucydides was not actively hostile to traditional religion; and indeed the attention which he devotes to Athens' 'purification' of Delos in 426/5 (III. 104 cf. I. 8. i) has prompted the suggestion that he was himself involved in that. Among the symptoms of savagery in the Corcyraean civil war were that 'men were dragged away from the sanctuaries and killed next to them; some men were even walled up in the sanctuary of Dionysus and died inside' (III. 81. v). In his Aetolian campaign of 426 the Athenian

Demosthenes camped in a sanctuary of Nemean Zeus (IV. 96. i), and then went on to a disastrous defeat (96–8). In their campaign against the Boeotians in 424/3 the Athenians occupied a sanctuary of Delian Apollo ('Delium'), put it to wholly secular uses (IV. 90. i–ii), suffered a disastrous defeat, and when the Boeotians complained about their use of the sanctuary they made a very cynical response:

> [A Boeotian herald to Athens proclaimed] that the Athenians were not acting rightly and were transgressing the institutions of the Greeks. For it was acknowledged by all that when they went against one another's territory they should keep away from the sanctuaries there; but the Athenians had fortified and were occupying Delium, and all that men do on unhallowed ground was happening there, and the water which was not to be touched by them except when used for purification for religious rites they were drawing and using as their water supply. ... The Athenians sent a herald of their own to the Boeotians, and said that they had not done any wrong to the sanctuary and would not intentionally do any damage in the future; for they had originally entered it not for that purpose but in order to resist from there those who rather were doing wrong to them. The custom of the Greeks was that whoever had the mastery of each territory, whether large or small, they should always possess the sanctuaries also, caring for them in a way close to what was customary in accordance with their ability. ... The water they had disturbed out of necessity, which they had not brought on themselves out of insolence, but when the Boeotians had taken the initiative in going against their own land they had been compelled in defending themselves to make use of it. (IV. 97. ii–98)

Here it seems likely that Thucydides at any rate regarded these failures to respect traditional customs as part of the decline in standards which occurred during the war, and the Athenian defeats as fitting if not brought about by the offended gods. As he observed in his discussion of civil war, 'war ... is a violent teacher' (III. 81. ii).

The priestess of Hera at Argos makes a formal appearance in II. 2. i when her forty-eighth year in the post is one of the three ways in which Thucydides dates the beginning of the war. More striking is his decision to report in IV. 133. ii–iii that in 422/1 this same priestess accidentally set fire to the temple and fled into exile, and another priestess was appointed. When the herms at Athens were damaged in 415, Thucydides gives a description of a kind which could be given equally by a believer and by an unbeliever:

> Meanwhile, of the herms in the city of Athens (in accordance with the local custom there are many of these, rectangular constructions, both in private porches and in sanctuaries) the majority had their faces cut about in a single night. (VI. 27. i)

And he says that the act was seen both as an omen for the Sicilian expedition and as a sign of a plot against the democracy (27. iii). He mentions other mutilations and the mock celebrations of the Eleusinian Mysteries, concluding again with the *motif* of an anti-democratic plot (28). When he returns to the subject later, he uses the verb cognate with *asebeia*, impiety, though without suggesting that he was himself particularly worried by impiety (53. i), and once more his emphasis is on a political plot (60. i, 61. i–iii).

Sophistic Contrasts

A contrast of which Thucydides makes a good deal of use is that between *logos* and *ergon*, 'word' and 'deed', or theory or appearance and reality. We have a version of this in his explanation of the Peloponnesian War: the 'grievances and disputes' which arose in the 430s were 'publicly mentioned', I assume by people other than Thucydides when they gave their accounts of how the war came about, while his 'truest reason', Athens' growing power and Sparta's fear of it, was 'most concealed in word' (I. 23. iv–vi).

There and in several other places Thucydides was proud of his ability to penetrate behind what was publicly said and was accepted by other people to what he saw as the contrasting reality. When the Spartan Pausanias returned to the Aegean after being recalled from his campaign of 478 to stand trial, he went 'in word for the Greeks' war (against Persia) but in deed to engage in negotiation with the King' (I. 128. iii). Periclean Athens was 'in word democracy but in deed rule by the first man' (II. 65. ix). Prisoners from Corcyra sent back there from Corinth were 'in word' ransomed but 'in deed they had undertaken to bring over Corcyra to Corinth' (III. 70. i). In Sicily in 415/14, when both Syracuse and Athens tried to gain its adhesion, Camarina decided 'in deed' to give some support to Syracuse though as little as possible, but 'in word' to give the same reply to both (VI. 88. i). In 413, when things were going badly for the Athenians in Sicily but Nicias still had hopes that Syracuse would be betrayed to them, 'in deed he was still undecided and continued thinking about it, but in his open word at the time he said he would not withdraw the force' (VII. 48. ii).

In Athens in 411, when opposition to the oligarchy of the Four Hundred grew, and Theramenes and Aristocrates placed themselves at the head of it, they said they were afraid of Athens' force at Samos (which had declared in favour of democracy), and of Alcibiades (who after his years in exile had joined that force), and that the envoys sent by the Four Hundred to Sparta (to try to negotiate an end to the war) might damage the city, and they called for the larger body of Five Thousand to be revealed 'in deed and not in name'. That was the political smokescreen of their *logos*, but in fact most of them were motivated by individual ambition (VIII. 89. ii–iii).

This mode of thinking can tempt people to suppose cynically that the reality is always different from the surface appearance, and Thucydides may sometimes have been inappropriately cynical. How could he know that Nicias was in fact wavering when he refused to leave Syracuse (Nicias was killed later that year)? Theramenes and Aristocrates no doubt were ambitious, but were they necessarily insincere in the fears which they expressed about the current state of affairs?

Thucydides does, however, have another formulation which allows him to have his cake and eat it. In I. 9. i Agamemnon led the Greeks against Troy 'because Agamemnon was foremost in power among his contemporaries, and not so much because he was leader of the suitors of Helen bound by the oaths of Tyndareus'. Books VI–VII give the impression that Athens' campaign in Sicily in 415–413 was misjudged in principle and its prospects were worsened by errors made on the spot, but in II. 65. xi Thucydides gives a different verdict: the reason was 'not so much' an error of judgment as failure to make the right supporting decisions in Athens (probably an allusion to the exile of Alcibiades after his involvement in the religious scandals of 415). After the Peace of Nicias Alcibiades 'did think that it was better that Athens should align itself with Argos, but he was also opposed (to the Peace) in pride and contentiousness', because in spite of his family's Spartan connections he had not been used in the making of it (V. 43. ii).

Contemporary Writers

As for the relationship between Thucydides and contemporary literature, it is clear that he is a product of the same intellectual world as other writers of his time, but it does not seem likely that he was directly influenced by them. One of the Sicilian envoys whose appeal led to Athens' war in Sicily in 427–424 was the orator Gorgias of Leontini (Diod. Sic. XII. 53). Thucydides does not mention him; and, while the prose style for which Gorgias became known involved sentences with precisely balanced clauses, Thucydides far more often wrote sentences with an element of balance but not a perfect balance. I 70. iii (in a speech by the Corinthians) provides an example:

> Again, they [the Athenians] are beyond their strength daring
>   and beyond their judgment risk-taking
>   and in dire straits optimistic;
> but your characteristic is short of your strength to act
>   and in your judgment not even in a secure position to trust
>   and of dire straits to think you will never be freed from them.

Similarities to Athenian tragedies of the later fifth century can be found not only in the kinds of argumentation used in his speeches but also in his passages of shorter dialogue, that with an Ambraciot herald in III. 113, that between Athenian and Boeotian heralds after the battle of Delium in IV. 97. ii–99, and the dialogue between Athenians and Melians in V. 85–111. And it has been pointed out that III. 113 gives us something resembling a recognition scene in tragedy. Thucydides would probably not have given his detailed description of the symptoms of Athens' plague (II. 49–50) if there had not been medical works which gave detailed accounts of illnesses, but he does not himself use the technical language which they use. His contrasts between *physis* and *nomos*, and between *logos* and *ergon*, are part of the repertoire of the sophists, but he shows no particular interest in contemporary philosophy. He never names a philosopher, not even Socrates, who is known from other texts to have fought in two of the battles which he reports, at Potidaea in 432 and at Delium in 424/3 (the politician Antiphon mentioned in VIII. 68. i, 90. i–ii, was probably not the same man as 'Antiphon the Sophist', though some scholars identify the two); and, if one of the considerations motivating those Athenians who favoured oligarchy in 411 was a philosophical view that oligarchy was in principle a better form of government than democracy, that is something which he does not mention.

There are similarities between things said by Thucydides and the *Athenian Constitution* of the 'Old Oligarch', a pamphlet preserved with the works of Xenophon, which argues perversely that democracy is bad in principle but appropriate to Athens and successful there (almost certainly it was not written by Xenophon and probably it is to be dated in the mid 420s). In both, for instance, we find the idea that Athens as the ruler of the sea almost has the advantageous position of being an island:

> If they come against our territory with infantry, we shall sail against theirs, and it will no longer be comparable for even a part of the Peloponnese to be laid waste and the whole of Attica: for they will not be able to take other land in return without fighting, but we have abundant land in the islands and on the mainland; for control of the sea is a great advantage. Consider. If we were islanders, who would be more invulnerable? (Pericles, in I. 143. iv–v)

> Furthermore, every mainland coast has either a projecting headland, or an offshore island, or some narrow strait; with the result that it is possible for the rulers of the sea to make a landing there, and to devastate the inhabitants of the mainland. But there is one thing which they lack. If the Athenians were thalassocrats who lived on an island, it would be possible for them to inflict damage, if they so wished, but, as long as they ruled the sea, not to suffer any, not to have their land ravaged and not to face the enemy's invasions. ([Xen.] *Athenian Constitution* ii. 13–14)

However, these are better explained by locating both writers in the same *milieu* than by supposing that either copied the other.

4

After Thucydides

In Antiquity

In recent decades the 'reception' of classical works in subsequent generations and in other cultures has become a major field for study, and the reception of Thucydides has been studied along with that of other authors. N. D. G. Morley has recently directed a major research project based in Bristol on Thucydides: Reception, Reinterpretation and Influence, and this is to be followed by one on Lessons of War: Reading Thucydides, 1914–45.

Thucydides himself remarked on his history's lack of superficial attractiveness (I. 22. iv: cf. p. 1). It does seem that in the centuries after his death he was less read than the more obviously attractive Herodotus; and another reason which has been suggested is that a long war between two Greek cities did not seem particularly relevant to the hellenistic and the Roman worlds. But this does not mean that he was neglected, or that he was without influence.

His account of the Peloponnesian War quickly became a classic, so that some fourth-century writers chose to start their histories at the point where his text ends. A surviving instance is Xenophon's *Hellenica* ('Greek affairs' from 411 to 362), where the juncture with Thucydides' text is imperfect: to the end of the Peloponnesian War he marked the beginnings of years in Thucydides' manner (though not the beginnings of winters also, and without numbering the years; further details have been added by an interpolator to the text which we have), but he has caused chronological problems by marking one new year fewer than he ought to have done. The unidentified author of the *Hellenica Oxyrhynchia* ('Greek affairs' found on papyrus at Oxyrhynchus in Egypt: in addition to the first-found fragment, on the mid 390s, we now have two shorter fragments, on the last years of the Peloponnesian War) marks the beginning of what is probably 396/5 with 'Those were the most substantial of the events which happened in Greece in this winter; at the beginning of the summer ... the eighth year began ... ' (9. i in the edition with translation of P. R. McKechnie and S. J. Kern; 12. i in the edition of M. H. Chambers) – which suggests that like Thucydides he recorded summers and winters, and that he continued Thucydides' numbering of years to the end of the war and then made a fresh start in 403/2. One later historian who used campaigning years, and the centrality of military history which they imply, was Hieronymus of Cardia, who dealt with the half-century after the death of Alexander the Great.

Influence of other kinds can be detected. Later knowledge of fifth-century history was not, of course, in every case obtained from Thucydides; but, of fourth-century Athenian orators, Apollodorus in the speech *Against Neaera* ([Demosthenes] LIX) in his account of Plataea in the early years of the Peloponnesian War clearly made use of Thucydides, though there are disagreements which point to his using another source as well (§§94–106: see Thuc. II. 2–6, 71–8, III. 20–4, 53–68). A passage on an episode in the *pentekontaetia* in Lysias' II. *Funeral Oration* is surely based on Thucydides (§§48–53: see Thuc. I. 105–6). Possibly Lysias' reference to Themistocles and the rebuilding of Athens' walls after the Persian Wars (XII. *Against Eratosthenes* 63: see Thuc. I. 91–3), and more certainly the details in Lycurgus' account of the death of the Spartan regent Pausanias (*Against Leocrates* 128–9: see Thuc. I. 128–34), are derived from Thucydides.

The military writer Aeneas Tacticus used Thucydides for the episode at Plataea in spring 431 (2. iii–vi), and also, more strikingly, repeated a remark included by Thucydides in a speech by the Spartan Brasidas before the battle outside Amphipolis in 422 (38. ii: see Thuc. V. 9. viii). What the philosophers Plato and Aristotle say about civil dissension is influenced by the discussion which Thucydides attaches to the dissension in Corcyra (with Thuc. II. 82–3 cf. Pl. *Resp.* VIII, Arist. *Pol.* IV. 1296 B 13–1297 A 13). Theopompus, another historian who began his Greek history where Thucydides ended (*FGrH* 115 T 19, F 5), tried to improve on one passage in Thucydides' version of Pericles' Funeral Oration (*FGrH* 115 F 395: see Thuc. II. 45. i). The author of the Aristotelian *Athenian Constitution* used Thucydides together with other sources on the assassination of Hipparchus in 514 and on the Athenian oligarchies of 411–410 (18 cf. Thuc. I. 20. ii, VI. 54-9; 29–33 cf. Thuc. VIII. 63. iii–98).

Of historians of the hellenistic period (between the death of Alexander the Great and the Roman conquest of the Greek world), two seem particularly Thucydidean. Hieronymus of Cardia (whose text does not survive but was the main source on Greek history of Diodorus Siculus XVIII–XX) was like Thucydides a serious and able historian; he used campaigning years (cf. above), did not invoke divine explanations of human events but did have some room for *tyche*, 'fortune', and did search for more fundamental causes of (for instance) the Lamian War of 323–322, and when he had a choice he did prefer the lower and more credible of competing statistics.

Polybius lived from the beginning of the second century to c. 118, and wrote a history to recount and explain the rise of Rome to dominate the Greek world, originally between 220 and 168, but extended to range from 264 to 146 (we have the first five of his 40 books, and 'fragments' of the remainder). He too was a serious historian, and he was aware at any rate of Thucydides' methodological statements (III. 31. ii cf. Thuc. I. 22. iv; III. 6–7 cf. Thuc. I. 23. iv–vi), yet surprisingly when he criticises Timaeus' version of the speech delivered by Hermocrates of Syracuse in 424 at the meeting which ended the war in which Athens had been intervening, he says nothing about Thucydides' version of that speech (XII. 25k–26: see Thuc. IV. 59–64). He preferred 'pragmatic' history (political and military, and useful to men in public life) to 'tragic' history (e.g. II. 63; 'pragmatic', e.g. I. 2. viii); he emphasised the importance of truth (e.g. I. 14. vi), but granted that reports of miracles could support the piety of the many if they did not go too far (XVI. 12. iii–xi), and that historians could be patriotic as long as that did not lead them into falsehood (XVI. 14. vi).

By the first century B.C. Thucydides' history was well known in Rome; and a striking use of it is the account of Athens' plague in the *De Rerum Natura* ('on the nature of things') of the philosophical poet Lucretius (VI. 1138–1286: see Thuc. II. 47. iii–54). Cicero used him as a source for fifth-century Athenian oratory, but he did not regard the style of his speeches as a suitable model to be followed (e.g. *De Oratore* II. 56, 93, *Brutus* 287), and indeed complained of their 'obscure and hidden meanings' (*Orator* 30). Similar complaints were made by the scholar Dionysius of Halicarnassus (e.g. *On Thucydides* 29–33, criticising Thuc. III. 82–3 on civil dissension), though he regarded Thucydides as the best historian (*On Thucydides* 2).

The historian Sallust (of whose works there survive the short *Catiline* and *Jugurtha* but only 'fragments' of the *Histories*) was widely recognised as having modelled himself on Thucydides (e.g. Livy *ap.* Sen. *Controv.* IX. i. 13–14, Vell. Pat. II. 36. ii). In particular he seems to have aimed at a Latin equivalent of Thucydides' style; and beyond human explanations for action he recognised only 'fortuna'. His debate between Cato and Caesar on the punishment of the Catilinarians has been compared to Thucydides' debate between Cleon and Diodotus on the punishment of Mytilene (*Cat.* 50–5: see Thuc. III. 36–49); and *Jugurtha* 41–2 digresses on the collapse of standards at Rome as Thucydides digresses on the collapse of standards in civil dissension (see Thuc. III. 82–3).

Under the Roman principate Quintilian was another writer who commented on Thucydides' style (e.g. 'dense and brief and always pressing upon himself', X. i. 73). Plutarch, when writing to expose *The Malice of Herodotus*, by contrast praised Thucydides for his restraint, even on Cleon and Hyperbolus (855 c, cf. 855 f, 870 d); while Lucian described him as 'the man who legislated for history' (*Hist. Conscr.* 42). The Jewish historian Josephus in his *Jewish War* modelled himself on Thucydides, writing for lovers of truth rather than of pleasure (I. 30); and his blaming the Jews' defeat not so much on Rome's military strength as on their own internal divisions was inspired by Thucydides' verdict on Athens' defeat in the Peloponnesian War (I. 9–12: see Thuc. II. 65. xi–xii). Tacitus, who developed his own manner of brevity and of pessimism, also knew and could make use of Thucydides (Thuc. III. 62. iii in *Ann.* VI. 42; other possible echoes are of III. 53. ii in *Ann.* I. 6, III. 67. vi in *Ann.* 52, III. 82. ii in *Ann.* IV. 60). Much later Procopius, who wrote about Justinian in the sixth century, often echoed Thucydides, for instance when reporting the bubonic plague in Constantinople in 542–3 (*De Bello Persico*, II. xxii–xxiii).

Byzantium, Renaissance

Scholars of the Byzantine period, like scholars of the Roman period, knew Thucydides, and they regarded him as 'the writer' *par excellence*, but found his writing obscure (e.g. Phot. *Bibl.* i. 105. 30–4 Henry). In particular Johannes Tzetzes, in the twelfth century, when annotating one of the oldest manuscripts of Thucydides now surviving, complained that the Athenians ought not to have exiled him to Thrace but to have thrown him into the abyss, because he 'hid through the darkness and woodenness of his language what time has brought on'; he wrote 'distorted and twisted sentences' (cited by D. R.

Reinsch in A. Rengakos and A. Tsakmakis [eds], *Brill's Companion to Thucydides*, 757–8). Thucydides was one of the models who contributed to the 'atticist' style of Greek used by some writers, but after the seventh century he was not directly imitated until the end of the Byzantine period.

Michael Choniates, archbishop of Athens at the end of the twelfth century, knew and in one of his letters assumed that the recipient knew Thucydides' account of the plague at Athens (*Ep.* 32). John Cantacuzenus was emperor 1347–54 and afterwards author of a *History* of his own times; and he adapted Thucydides' account of the plague in his own account of the plague which afflicted Europe in 1347–8 (IV. 8). Michael Critobulus, fifteenth-century author of a *History* of the rise of the Ottomans, in his first long speech of Sultan Mehmed (I. 14–16) drew on Pericles' two speeches in Thucydides II and on the Corinthians' contrast between Athens and Sparta in book I. In Mehmed's next speech (I. 48–51) he used Phormio's speech to the Athenian navy in the Gulf of Corinth and Brasidas' speech to his soldiers at Amphipolis (Thuc. II. 89, V. 9) – and Arrian's speech of Alexander the Great before the battle of Gaugamela in 331 (Arr. *Anab.* III. 5–8). In the battle for Constantinople Mehmed's reaction to the withdrawal of the Genoese Guistiniani echoes Brasidas' reaction to the withdrawal of Cleon from Amphipolis (I. 60. i: see Thuc. V. 10. v). The Peloponnesian siege of Plataea (Thuc. II. 71–8) is pressed into service on two occasions (I. 33, 34). For a plague at Constantinople in 1467 (V. 17–18) he used both Thucydides and Procopius.

In western Europe there was a period when Thucydides and other Greek writers were known only from references to them by Latin writers. Petrarch, for instance, in the fourteenth century, knew of Thucydides and his exile from the *Natural History* of Pliny (*Rerum Memorandarum Libri* II. 33: see Plin. *H.N.* VII. 11). Direct knowledge of Thucydides first appears when Juan Fernández de Heredia was Master of the Knights Hospitallers in Rhodes from 1379 to 1382, after which he ended his life in Avignon. He acquired Greek manuscripts in Rhodes, and had a number of texts translated into Aragonese, including 38 speeches from Thucydides – but his work remained unknown and did not influence subsequent developments.

More important for the knowledge of Greek and of Greek literature was the appointment of Manuel Chrysoloras to teach Greek at Florence (1397–1400), after which he taught elsewhere in Italy. At the beginning of the fifteenth century Thucydides was being read by Pier Paolo Vergerio, who taught at Padua and Florence. Leonardo Bruni, who translated many Greek works into Latin, declined an invitation to translate Thucydides, but used Thucydides as a model for his *History of the Florentine People* and Pericles' Funeral Oration in Thuc. II. 35–46 as a model for a speech of his own. Other historians later in the century claimed to use Thucydides as a model: for instance Poggio Bracciolini planned to write a history of Venice imitating Thucydides and Xenophon; and Marcantonio Coccio Sabellico wrote a universal history, *Enneades sive Rhapsodia Historiarum*, in which his account of the Peloponnesian War was based directly on Thucydides (III. v–viii).

A complete Latin translation of Thucydides was made between 1448 and 1452, as part of the project of Pope Nicholas V to have the whole of Greek literature translated, by Lorenzo Valla, best known for his exposure as a forgery of the 'Donation of Constantine' (a document in which the emperor Constantine donated the western Roman empire to the Roman church). This remains important for the text of Thucydides, because he had access to one or more manuscripts independent of those which survive now. The first printed edition of the Greek text was published in 1502 by Aldo Manuzio at his Aldine Press in Venice: the Press was founded in 1494; its first Greek authors were Theocritus (1495) and Aristotle (1495–8); Herodotus also was published in 1502. The first more scholarly edition of Thucydides was by Henri Estienne (Stephanus), along with editions of various other Greek authors: his Thucydides was originally published in 1564 and revised in 1588; it included a commentary which was primarily linguistic.

At first Thucydides was not a popular author, because of the difficulty of his Greek and his lack of moralising. Niccolò Machiavelli, active in politics and writing about politics in the early sixteenth century, may have owed a little to Thucydides but was not strongly influenced by him. However, the Italian diplomat Giovanni della Casa made Latin translations of speeches and of the account of the Athenian plague; and in Germany the Lutheran Philipp Melanchthon when professor of Greek at Wittenberg lectured on Thucydides and wrote about him, and produced his own Latin translation of speeches and some other parts of the text. Other sixteenth-century scholars also produced editions, translations and commentaries; and at the end of the century Fabio Paolino da Udine was prompted by contemporary plagues to comment on Thucydides' plague.

The first vernacular translation of Thucydides was into French, was made not from the Greek text but from Valla's Latin translation, by Claude de Seyssel, and was completed in 1527. An English translation by Thomas Nichols, based on de Seyssel's French translation, was published in 1550. The first translation into English from the Greek text was by the political philosopher Thomas Hobbes, whose *Leviathan* was published in 1651 (during the Civil War, which the royalist Hobbes spent in exile). His Thucydides was published in 1628 and was his first publication. He greatly admired Thucydides, and in his Preface described him as 'the most politic historiographer that ever writ'; he judged that Thucydides 'least of all liked the democracy' and 'best approved of the regal government', and he himself believed that with no supranational laws or bodies to enforce them relations between states were 'in the condition of perpetual war' (*Leviathan* §21).

More Recently

What we may think of as more modern approaches to Thucydides, combined with praise of him as a superlative historian, began in the late eighteenth century and came to fruition in nineteenth-century Germany. B. G. Niebuhr was a financier who in 1810 retired from public life to become a professor in Berlin; he served as Prussian ambassador to Rome from 1816 to 1823, but returned to academic work after that, and revised and continued the *Roman History* which he had begun in Berlin. He considered Thucydides 'the first real and true historian', and the Peloponnesian War 'the most immortal of all wars, because it is described by the greatest of all historians that ever lived'. What he admired were Thucydides' thoroughness and intelligence, his perception of historical reality, and the vivid writing based on his having lived through the events which he recorded. Niebuhr in turn is praised by Arnold (below), who said that he 'has not so much written a perfect history himself, as he has pointed out the true means by which it may be written' (Arnold, *Thucydides*, i, p. xi).

L. von Ranke studied at Leipzig and from 1825 taught history at the University of Berlin, as professor from 1834 to 1871; he attached importance to the critical use of historical sources, and to teaching in seminars. His claim (in his *Histories of the Roman and German Peoples from 1494 to 1535*, i [1824], p. vi) to have written 'wie es eigentlich gewesen' ('how it actually was'), whatever he may himself have meant by that, has been taken as emblematic of the kind of history which purports to 'let the facts speak for themselves' rather than to impose a pattern of interpretation on them. In his student days he wrote a thesis on Thucydides, and late in his life he expressed his admiration of him: while Herodotus wrote of a past which was accessible only through memory, Thucydides wrote of his own time, dealing rationally with human activities, treating the two sides in the war dispassionately, and with vivid powers of description. Here we have the origin of the view of Thucydides which is impressed by his authoritative manner and his remarks on the trouble he has taken to get the facts right, and which sees him as an energetic and critical searcher for and an objective reporter of truth, which became the dominant view of him until the middle of the twentieth century.

In Britain T. B. Macaulay admired Thucydides more and more as his life progressed, primarily for his artistry in narration, 'producing an effect on the imagination, by skilful selection and disposition, without indulging in the license of invention', but at first he considered him not 'a really philosophical historian' (review of H. Neele, *England* [in the Romance of History series], *Edinburgh Review* xciv [May 1828], 331–67 at 339, 341, published anonymously = *Life and Works of Lord Macaulay* [Edinburgh Edition. London: Longmans, 1897], v. 122–61 at 131, 133). T. Arnold, the celebrated headmaster of Rugby School, wrote more on Roman history than on Greek, but his works included an annotated edition of Thucydides, in which he claimed credit particularly for his topographical notes (first edition 1830–5). G. Grote, who with Macaulay was among the first people in the modern world to view democracy positively rather than negatively, took his democratic enthusiasm to the extent of criticising Thucydides for excessive hostility to Cleon; but that was merely a qualification of his overall view that 'in the case of Thucydidês, the qualities necessary to the historiographer, in their application to recent events, have been developed with a degree of perfection never since surpassed' (*History of Greece* [first published 1846–56], ch. lii on Pylos, ch. liv on Amphipolis, ch. xvi overall judgment). 'In brief, the majority of nineteenth-century historians were able to recognise him as one of their own' (N. D. G. Morley, *Thucydides and the Idea of History*, 31).

A notable exception to the view of Thucydides as supremely rational and objective was a book published in 1907, F. M. Cornford's *Thucydides Mythistoricus*. Starting from a belief that Thucydides' account of the causes of the Peloponnesian War was mistaken (Pericles was forced into the war by his commercial supporters who wanted to capture the trade with the west), he concluded that Thucydides 'had not reckoned with the truth that you cannot collect facts, like so many pebbles, without your own personality and the common mind of your age and country having something to say to the choice and arrangement of the collection', and that, while every one of his facts might be correct, Thucydides' presentation of his material was shaped by an essentially tragic view of history.

While inscriptions made historians increasingly aware of things which Thucydides might have mentioned but did not, the consensus was undisturbed, and continued to see in Thucydides 'an ideal of absolute and rigidly tested truth' (J. H. Finley, *Thucydides* [1942], 105). The article on Thucydides written for the first edition of the *Oxford Classical Dictionary* (1949) by H. T. Wade-Gery (with a concluding section on style by J. D. Denniston), which praised 'his singular truthfulness', has been retained in the third (1996) and fourth (2012) editions, but with an addtional section by S. Hornblower on more recent work (see in the fourth edition 'Thucydides [2]', 472–7). But, while Cornford's economic reason for the Peloponnesian War has found no recent supporters, his assumption that Thucydides must have been formed by his context and that he did not simply chronicle facts but presented them in a particular way has since the middle of the twentieth century increasingly been accepted. Our world is a world of uncertainties rather than certainty, and the notion that even Thucydides could objectively and dispassionately discover and report the truth (even if he himself thought or claimed that he could) is nowadays considered impossible.

Marxists accused of bias replied that everybody is biased, and that those who do not admit to their bias are worse than those who do – and indeed Thucydides, in view of his family background, his support for Pericles in spite of that background, and his own career as an Athenian general exiled for his failure, must himself have held strong views which will have affected his understanding of the history of his time. 'Post-modernists' insisted that history is not 'out there', simply waiting to be discovered, but is made by those who find it and write it, and indeed it is remade again and again by those who read what historians have written. But against extreme versions of these approaches it has to be replied that, although individuals do indeed to some extent make history, what distinguishes history from fiction is that we are not free to make it up however we wish: we may be more sophisticated and more aware of certain kinds of problems than our predecessors, but it remains true that in writing or in reading history we are trying to discover and make sense of what actually happened, not simply conjuring up what we should like to have happened.

Nevertheless in recent scholarship Thucydides the objective chronicler has become Thucydides the artful reporter (the title of V. J. Hunter's 1973 book, *Thucydides, the Artful Reporter*, is conveniently emblematic of the change in fashion), and more recent studies of Thucydides have been increasingly concerned to discuss, from a variety of viewpoints, not all mutually exclusive, how and with what purpose(s) Thucydides has crafted his narrative. For instance, Hunter's book sought to show how Thucydides presented his material in order to bring out patterns in history, and argued that his ascriptions of plans and motives were inferred from what was actually done. H. R. Rawlings, III, in *The Structure of Thucydides' History* (1981), saw parallels between the first half of the Peloponnesian War and the second half, and in the light of that suggested how the end of the war might have been treated in 'books IX–X'. W. R. Connor wrote his *Thucydides* (1984) as an unsettled man who had lost the old certainties, and who worked his way through the text on the assumption that Thucydides was seeking not to state his own views explicitly but 'to draw the reader in, to awaken our critical and evaluative faculties'.

S. Hornblower and others have brought to Thucydides the insights of narratology, the study of techniques used in the presentation of the narrative, such as focalisation (seeing particular episodes from the viewpoint of particular people), narrative displacement (making an item more or less conspicuous by mentioning it at a point other than the point which would be expected), presentation through negation (as when in I. 104. iv Thucydides says that the Athenians 'did not disturb the force in Aegina': cf. pp. 32–3), and the function of 'narrator interventions' in a text in which the story otherwise 'tells itself' (e.g. II. 65. v–xiii on Pericles and his successors).

Such approaches have inevitably cast doubt on the view that Thucydides was supremely conscientious and reliable as a recorder of truth. As early as 1965 K. J. Dover, who seems now to belong to the earlier rather than the more recent school of interpreters, was moved to write in the Prefaces of his small editions of books VI and VII:

> Anyone who believes that Thucydides was omniscient, dispassionate, and infinitely wise, and that there is nothing to be said on the other side of any question on which Thucydides has made a pronouncement, may find some of my comments irreverent and cynical. I offer no apology.

A. J. Woodman, in a chapter in his *Rhetoric in Classical Historiography* (1988), concentrated on Thucydides as a writer of historical literature rather than an investigator of history, and (for instance) wondered whether by following a tradition which connected war and plague 'Thucydides magnifed the plague [at Athens] out of all proportion to its real significance'. E. Badian, in one of the articles revised in his *From Plataea to Potidaea* (1993), argued that in his account of the origin of the Peloponnesian War Thucydides was writing as a dishonest journalist, distorting the facts to support his case. While most readers would not go so far in doubting Thucydides' facts, it is better that we should read him with the possibility of doubt in our minds than in a spirit of uncritical trust.

Added to such doubts about Thucydides as a recorder of truth, there has been a growing interest among historians in questions very different from Thucydides' narrow focus on fighting with a minimum of politics. If to nineteenth-century historians Thucydides was 'one of their own' (above), by the end of the twentieth century historians were more likely to insist that 'Thucydides is not a colleague' (translated from the title of an article in French by N. Loraux, *Quaderni di Storia* vi 1980, 55–81).

Beyond Classics

In previous centuries, in the European tradition classics was an essential element in education, and it does not need to be explained why the diplomat della Casa translated parts of Thucydides and the political philosopher Hobbes translated the whole. It reflects the continuing importance of classics in education that in the First World War passages from Pericles' Funeral Oration were displayed on London's buses (e.g. 'We have more at stake than those who have no such inheritance. If we sing the glories of our country, it was the warriors and their like who have set hand to array her', II. 43. i–ii). More recently, the 2003 Draft Treaty Establishing a Constitution for Europe began its Preamble by quoting 'Our Constitution … is called a democracy because power is in the hands not of a minority but of the greatest number' (II. 37. i); and Sir Ivor Roberts, British Ambassador to Italy, in his valedictory telegram in 2006 quoted from the Melian dialogue 'The strong do what they can: the weak suffer what they must' (V. 89).

In today's world education is divided into many separate disciplines, of which classics is only one, and is a discipline which plays little or no part in the education of many people. But Thucydides has been influential in other disciplines as well as in classics. Military historians, including those in military academies, have made use of his military narrative. Specialists in politics and political theory have focused on his treatment of different political regimes and of civil dissension. And his history has been seized on by students of international relations (the world's first professor of international politics, A. E. Zimmern, appointed at Aberystwyth in 1919, had begun his academic career as an ancient historian), and particularly by those who have seen themselves as Realists in opposition to Idealists and who have seen Thucydides as giving a Realist portrayal of Greek inter-state relations, in which states which had power exercised it without compunction, and aimed to increase their power rather than to act in accordance with agreed standards.

The Peloponnesian War was indeed a great war in terms of its length and of the numbers of states and of individuals caught up in it, but it did not definitively resolve the rivalry between Athens and Sparta. That continued into the fourth century, and was resolved when the Thebans defeated the Spartans overwhelmingly on land at Leuctra in 371 – after which Athens and Sparta became allies against Thebes until Athens and Thebes combined to resist Philip II of Macedon but were defeated by him at Chaeronea in 338.

Thucydides' history of the Peloponnesian War is a great history because of his punctiliousness in trying to establish the facts and his seriousness and intelligence in explaining them – and because he combined these purposes of establishment and explanation in such a way as to reflect on and prompt his readers to reflect on issues of lasting importance. It was surely because of his own consciousness of this that he declared his history to be a 'possession for all time' (I. 22. iv: cf. p. 1). It is, as people say, supremely 'good to think with', and fully deserving to be read not only by those who make a study of ancient Greece but by all who are interested in the behaviour of states and of individuals.

Further Reading

Texts, Translations, Commentaries

A Greek text of Thucydides is published in the Oxford Classical Texts series (Oxford University Press: edited by H. Stuart Jones; critical apparatus revised by J. E. Powell; index revised; a new Oxford text edited by G. Liberman is in preparation); also with English translation in the Loeb Classical Library (Harvard University Press: edited by C. F. Smith) and with French translation in the Budé series (Collection des Universités de France, Paris: Les Belles Lettres: edited by J. de Romilly et al.).

A nineteenth-century English translation which has become a classic is that of R. Crawley (1876), republished in various series in a version slightly revised by R. C. Feetham; a further revision of that translation is included, together with introduction, notes and appendixes by various scholars, in R. B. Strassler (ed.), *The Landmark Thucydides* (New York: Free Press, 1996). The Penguin Classics translation by R. Warner, to which M. I. Finley later added an introduction and some notes (Harmondsworth: Penguin, 1954; revised 1972), was one of the early volumes in the series, when the policy was to tell the story in fluent English without worrying about finer details. Among more recent translations is that in the Oxford World's Classics series by M. Hammond, for which I have provided the introduction and notes (Oxford University Press, 2009). Other recent translations are by W. Blanco (New York: Norton, 1998), inclining to fluent English; S. Lattimore (Indianapolis: Hackett, 1998), and J. Mynott (Cambridge University Press, 2013), both inclining to faithful reproduction of Thucydides' Greek.

There are two major commentaries on Thucydides: A. W. Gomme, A. Andrewes, K. J. Dover, *A Historical Commentary on Thucydides*

(Oxford University Press, 1945–81); and, more up-to-date and also more accessible to those who cannot read Greek, S. Hornblower, *A Commentary on Thucydides* (Oxford University Press, 1991–2008). Shorter and simpler is D. Cartwright, *A Historical Commentary on Thucydides: A Companion to Rex Warner's Penguin Translation* (University of Michigan Press, 1997).

Annotated editions of individual books from the late nineteenth and early twentieth centuries, by E. C. Marchant and C. E. Graves (London: Macmillan), are still in use; and editions of books VI and VII were published by K. J. Dover (Oxford University Press, 1965). I have published editions of books I, II, III and IV. 1–V. 24, with introduction, translation and commentaries focusing primarily on the subject matter (Warminster: Aris and Phillips → Oxford: Oxbow, 1988–2014); and J. S. Rusten has published an edition of book II, and will shortly publish an edition of book I, with introduction and commentaries with a greater emphasis on the language (Cambridge University Press, 1989/forthcoming).

Other Books

The Peloponnesian War and the *pentekontaetia*, the half-century of Athenian expansion which preceded it, are covered in all standard histories of classical Greece. There are also by D. Kagan a four-volume history – *The Outbreak of the Peloponnesian War*, *The Archidamian War*, *The Peace of Nicias and the Sicilian Expedition*, *The Fall of the Athenian Empire* (Cornell University Press, 1969–87); combined in a single e-book under the title *New History of the Peloponnesian War* (2012) – and a one-volume history, *The Peloponnesian War: Athens and Sparta in Savage Conflict, 431–404 B.C.* (New York: Viking, 2003). G. E. M. de Ste. Croix, *The Origins of the Peloponnesian War* (London: Duckworth, 1972), ranges far more widely than its title suggests and often challenges accepted views. G. L. Cawkwell, *Thucydides and the Peloponnesian War* (London: Routledge, 1997), is shorter and less formidable, but again willing to challenge the consensus.

On Thucydides J. H. Finley, *Thucydides* (Harvard University Press, 1942), is the best of the older general books. S. Hornblower, *Thucydides* (London: Duckworth, 1987), is the best of the newer general books; and he has collected a series of his articles on Thucydides in his *Thucydidean Themes* (Oxford University Press, 2011). K. J. Dover, *Thucydides* (*Greece & Rome*: New Surveys in the Classics vii 1973), is a succinct review of various topics but was published too early to reflect more recent literary interests.

Chapters from various viewpoints by various authors are assembled in A. Rengakos and A. Tsakmakis (eds), *Brill's Companion to Thucydides* (Leiden: Brill, 2006); J. S. Rusten (ed.), *Thucydides* (Oxford Readings in Classical Studies. Oxford University Press, 2009); and P. A. Low (ed.), *Oxford Handbook to Thucydides* (Oxford University Press), is in preparation.

On the reception of Thucydides there are five chapters in *Brill's Companion to Thucydides*. The research project based in Bristol has yielded K. C. Harloe and N. D. G. Morley (eds), *Thucydides and the Modern World: Reception, Reinterpretation and Influence from the Renaissance to the Present* (Cambridge University Press, 2012); N. D. G. Morley, *Thucydides and the Idea of History* (London: I. B. Tauris, 2014); C. Lee and N. D. G. Morley (eds), *A Handbook to the Reception of Thucydides* (Chichester: Wiley–Blackwell, 2015).

Books published on Thucydides in recent decades are so many and so varied that any short selection would be somewhat arbitrary. I limit myself below to giving details of other modern works which I have had occasion to cite in this book:

Badian, E. *From Plataea to Potidaea* (Johns Hopkins University Press, 1993).

Connor, W. R. *Thucydides* (Princeton University Press, 1984).
Cornford, F. M. *Thucydides Mythistoricus* (London: Arnold, 1907).
Finley, J. H. *Thucydides* (Harvard University Press, 1942).
Hunter, V. J. *Thucydides, the Artful Reporter* (Toronto: Hakkert, 1973).
Rawlings, H. R., III, *The Structure of Thucydides' History* (Princeton University Press, 1981).
Woodman, A. J. *Rhetoric in Classical Historiography* (London: Croom Helm, 1988).

Index

Aegina 26–7, 32–3
Aetolia 43, 64–5
Alcibiades, of Athens 44, 46–7, 54, 67–8
Ambracia 29, 42, 44, 69
Amphipolis 18, 52, 76
Argos 4, 12, 45, 65–6, 68
artistry *see* facts and artistry
Athens *passim*, esp. 3–6, 9, 36; *see also* Delian League; Piraeus; names of individual Athenians

Boeotia 26, 42, 45, 65, 69; *see also* Thebes
Brasidas, of Sparta 18, 47, 72–3, 76
bronze age 2–3; *see also* Trojan War

causes of Peloponnesian War 26–7, 35
Cimon, of Athens 8, 54
Cleon, of Athens 18, 21–2, 28, 44, 47–8, 54, 58, 74, 80
composition of Thucydides' history 13–14
Corcyra 17–18, 27–9, 48, 56, 67, 73
Corinth 20, 27–8, 32–3, 39, 45–6, 48, 67
Corinth, Gulf of (battles in 429) 23–4, 37, 39

Decelea 13, 26, 29, 31, 34
Delian League 5, 29–30, 57–9
Delium (battle in 424/3) 65, 69
Delos 5, 32, 36, 64
democracy 5, 53–5
   in Argos 45
   in Athens 5, 9, 31–2, 67
Demosthenes, of Athens 42, 52, 64–5
Dionysius, of Halicarnassus, writer 11, 74

Eleusinian Mysteries 17, 66

facts and artistry 16–18, 32–3, 36, 46, 49, 79–83
finance 30–1
focalisation 45–6
funeral of Athens' war dead 25, 61, 73, 77, 84

Gorgias, of Leontini 68
Gylippus, of Sparta 46, 52

Hellenica Oxyrhynchia 72
helots, of Sparta 10
Heraclea 33–4
herms, in Athens 17, 66
Herodotus, of Halicarnassus, historian 7, 16, 35, 52–3, 60
Hieronymus, of Cardia, historian 72–3
Hobbes, T. 39, 78
Homer, poet of *Iliad* and *Odyssey* 6, 17, 35–6, 47
Hyperbolus, of Athens 44, 54

Mantinea (battle in 418) 12–13, 16–17, 24–5, 32, 41, 43
Marathon (battle in 490) 4, 8, 25
Megara 26–8, 41, 48
Melos 22, 40, 58, 69
Messenia 43–4; *see also* Pylos
Miltiades, of Athens 8
morality 55–9
Mytilene 20–2, 37, 40, 45–6, 58, 74

narratology 45–8, 83
natural phenomena 33, 43, 60, 62–4
negation 32–3
Nicias, of Athens 18, 44, 52, 54, 62, 67

Nicias, Peace of (421) 12, 14, 68

Old Oligarch *see* Xenophon
oligarchy 5, 53–5
    in Athens (411–410) 18, 31–2, 34, 44, 55, 67–8, 93
oracles 32–3, 60, 62, 64

Pausanias, of Sparta 35, 44, 67, 72
Peloponnesian League 4–5, 48
pentekontaetia 11, 72
Pericles, of Athens 28, 40, 44, 54–5, 57, 81–3
    speeches 12, 20, 30, 47–8, 58, 61–2, 73, 76–7, 84
perioikoi, of Sparta 10
Persia 4–5, 7, 13, 16, 24, 35, 60; *see also* Tissaphernes
philosophy 6–7, 59–60; *see also* sophists
Phormio, of Athens 23–4, 47
Piraeus 12, 37, 45
plague, at Athens 39, 41–3, 51, 56, 61–2, 64, 69, 75–6
Plataea 16, 37–9, 46, 72, 76
polis 3
political views of Thucydides 53–5
Polybius, of Megalopolis, historian 73–4
Potidaea 27, 60, 69
Pylos 18, 28, 37, 39, 41, 45, 54

reception of Thucydides
    Byzantine 75–6
    Greek 71–4
    modern 79–85
    Renaissance 76–9
    Roman 74–5
religion 32–4, 55–7, 59–66; *see also* Eleusinian Mysteries; herms; oracles

Scione 16
Sicily 13, 14, 23, 36–7, 40–1, 43, 45–6, 58, 67–8
sophists 8, 55–6. 66–8
sources of Thucydides' information 14–18, 35–6
Sparta *passim*, esp. 3–6, 9–10, 31–2, 36; *see also* helots; Peloponnesian League; *perioikoi*; names of individual Spartans
speeches 19–22, 57–9, 73–4; *see also* names of individual speakers
stasis (civil dissension) 39, 51–2, 56–7, 74
superlatives 43
Syracuse *see* Sicily

Tacitus, Roman historian 21, 75
Thebes 16, 53
Themistocles, of Athens 16, 35, 44, 55, 72
Thucydides son of Melesias, of Athens, grandfather of historian 8, 54
Thucydides son of Olorus, of Athens, historian *passim*
    life and career 8, 15, 18, 21, 31, 52, 75–6
Tissaphernes, Persian satrap 16, 31, 47
tragedy 6, 22, 69
Trojan War 6, 35, 68
tyche (fortune) 60–3, 74
tyranny 47–8, 57

Xenophon, of Athens, writer 13, 71–2
    Athenian Constitution attributed to him 69–70